IMPROVING YOUR MEMORY

THE UNIQUE 5 X 5 SYSTEM

Peter Marshall

Key To Books

SELF-DEVELOPMENT

IMPROVINGYOUR MEMORY

The unique 5 x 5 system

Dr Peter Marshall

Key To Books

British Library Cataloguing in Publication Data
A catalogue record of this book is available from the British Library.

Published by Key To Books 2012.

Key To Books is an imprint of Oakley Books Ltd., 10 Buckhurst Road, Bexhill on Sea, East Sussex, TN40 1QF.

Note: the material contained in this book is set out in good faith for general guidance and no liability can be accepted for loss or expense incurred as a result of relying in particular circumstances on statements made in the book. The laws and regulations are complex and liable to change and readers should check the current position with the relevant authorities before making personal arrangements.

Cover design by Pentacor Design.
Printed and bound in Exeter by Imprint Digital.

1

Contents

Preface

Preface

It is now well established that long- and short-term memory are different processes and both can be enhanced with the right techniques.

This system is easy to learn and the potential for memory improvement is huge — not just marginal; we are talking multiplication. It is quite feasible to enhance the power of the memory many, many fold. This book is a simple, plain English treatment of the *Five x Five System,* which I designed for memory research purposes and which I have tested over and over again in my memory-training courses on people of all ages. It has attracted much publicity on TV and radio.

We are our memories. In the 21st century people live on their wits. What determines how successful we are in whatever we do is our mental ability and, to a large extent, that depends on our memory quality. The author and colleagues of London University recently discovered that memory quality has even replaced IQ as the main predictor of one's educational outcome. Everything we do in life depends on memory quality.

There have been memory-enhancement courses around for many decades, many of them very good but, invariably, they have required an extended period of study — many weeks, and often months. Because of the nature of the research I was doing, I had to produce a course that could be learned quickly, so that large groups of people could be taught at low cost. The solution was to select a manageable number of core skills, giving more or less equal coverage to all the aspects of memory. The result is the *Five x five System* - combining the best of what has been known for centuries with what has been discovered in modern times, and with a few important new features not to be found elsewhere added.

Whatever your reasons for buying this book, whether you want to improve your social skills by remembering names and faces better, achieve total recall in your college exams, play better poker or bridge, learn a foreign language, remember jokes, learn actors' lines, or reverse the process of memory decline, this book will help you.

1

Preparing the Material

Before anything goes into your long-term memory it has to enter your short-term memory. This in itself is not guaranteed. What happens is that your perceptual process scans long-term memory to look for a pattern-match with what it is seeing, hearing, smelling, feeling or tasting. If it finds one, the material enters short-term memory and the first step towards long-term storage has been achieved.

But even here it is vulnerable. Short-term memory lasts for only between 15 and 30 seconds before the trace decays. For it to pass to long-term memory, where it can last for anything from minutes to a lifetime, it has to become the subject of meaningful thought. Added to this time-function decay, short-term memory is also affected by displacement. It has only a very small capacity. It's as if it has slots - seven of them - for the average person can handle only between five and nine simple bits of data in short-term memory. If new data enters short-term memory, it displaces data already there - *in one ear and out the other,* you might say.

Chunking

How can we make the best use of short-term memory? *Chunking* is the first principle of the *Five x Five System.* The five sub-principles you must learn are these:

- Chunk material you are trying to remember
- Build chunks themselves into a hierarchy
- Use six standard shapes for the chunks
- Use acronyms, if possible, to remember the details in the chunks
- Use acrostics where acronyms cannot be made

Although the short-term memory can only handle, on average, seven bits of data, each of these can be loaded with another seven and each of them with another seven, and so on. We can build the levels of the hierarchy as high as we like, for this is not a factor in memory potential. It is the number of bits at each level that is crucial - not the number of levels - so there really is no limit. To break the limitations of short-term memory capacity, you simply have to do a bit of preparation of the material before you begin to store it, then it's easy. Later you'll have the opportunity to try it for yourself.

Chunking numbers
If you're chunking six digit telephone numbers, you can chunk the sounds into two groups of three digits, so that instead of your inner voice hearing it as six digits, it hears it as two sounds, each of a run of three digits: 359, 215. Your inner voice will remember the echo of each of these groups as if it were a single pattern of sounds, like a short run of musical notes.

Seven digit telephone numbers are remembered best if they are read and rehearsed in groups of four, then three digits. The two resulting patterns stick in sensory memory better than the other way round.

Chunking cards
If you are trying to remember runs of playing cards, group them in 3's.

Chunking names and faces
You may have a lot of names and faces to remember. If so, there are various ways you can chunk them. The obvious way is in gender types - males and females, but that is likely to leave you with two groups too large for your short-term memory to handle. You can further chunk them by hair colour, age group, eyes, or some other characteristics, and go on subgrouping until no subgroup is larger than five. This is a level of chunking that more or less anybody can handle efficiently and it leaves a lot of thinking space available.

Chunking foreign languages
Learning a foreign language is a memory-taxing task. You can make things easier for yourself if you chunk words you learn each day into chunks of manageable size. Group them into nouns, pronouns, verbs, epithets, adjectives, adverbs, and so on.

Another way to group foreign language words is by context - holiday words, work words, educational words, and so on.

Remembering long numbers
If you are trying to remember a very long number, you're likely to be trying to impress someone, or going for a record. If it is the latter, let me tell you how it is done, at least at the short-term memory stage;

the long-term memory strategy will be revealed in Chapter 3.

The best way to chunk long numbers seems to be in chunks of five and each of these split into smaller chunks of two and three.

Chunking text

What if you have to remember a whole text? Some people have to. Some religious faiths (Judaism and Islam, for example) require their clerics to know the Scriptures word for word, including the exact position where each word appears on a page.

Actors are required to memorise long sections of lines. Then there are speeches. To be able to speak in public is a crucial social skill you have to develop if you want to get on.

All these can be easily achieved with the right technique. The first stage is to chunk the material before you even try to learn it.

The obvious first order of chunking in a text is into sentences. Next come paragraphs, then sections, and then chapters. You can anchor each sentence in your memory by its main point. Sentences have only a single main idea in them and it may be possible to express it in a single word. Each paragraph hangs together in some way and the pattern may be more or less the same in each one, for example, sentence 1 — the point, sentence 2 — elaboration, sentence 3 — evidence, and sentence 4 — implications. The paragraphs may not be entirely consistent throughout a text, but some degree of consistency may be discernible. If you spot it, you will save yourself an awful lot of mental work.

The same goes for sections. There may be some degree of consistency in paragraphic functions within each section.

Lastly, express in a single word or phrase the patterns that describe the make-up of the sections in each chapter, then the pattern that holds the chapters together into a whole book. That is often consistent across a wide range of books. For example, if they are the findings of a research project, they will contain a literature review, an introduction to the project, a methodology chapter, a findings chapter and a discussion chapter.

Exam revision

You may have already heard of, and may indeed use, the technique of *Successive Note Reduction*. This is an exam-revision method where you reduce each section of your notes to a single page, then each page to a paragraph, then each paragraph to a sentence, then each sentence to a phrase and, finally, each phrase to a key word. It is a very effective method of storing course material firmly in memory and the reason it works is the process of hierarchy building.

The myriad ideas are chunked down to a small number of mind-sized bites and the process of constructing the hierarchy lays the pathways between the parts more firmly than you will even be aware of. Your mind will pick them up easily. The reason the pathways are laid firmly is because the hierarchy construction requires a significant amount of semantic processing. Semantic code is the principal code in which long-term memories are stored.

Use shapes

What if you have a large number of categories of different sizes in your hierarchy? You might remember the structure, but how will you be sure you have remembered the number of items in each category? How will you know when you have recalled them all?

The answer is to use shapes and, in accordance with the rationale underlying the *Five x Five System,* I would suggest your categories should rarely be larger than five and never larger than six. Not only does this put less demand on short-term memory and leave free as much thinking space as possible, but also it is not quick
and easy to draw a memorable object with more than six vertices.

1 .   spot   ○
2 .   dumbbells   ○—○
3 .   triangle   △
4 .   square   ▢
5 .   star   ☆
6 .   hexagon   ⬡

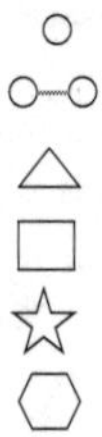

Figure 1. Shapes used in the Five x Five System

With these shapes you can construct a studygram. This is a complex of six different shapes, arranged in a format that has as much symmetry as possible, so that it is memorable.

Let's look at an example.

Imagine you're a student of commerce and you have to remember these facts:

- Categories of production - primary, secondary and tertiary
- Division of labour - advantages, disadvantages and levels
- Types of economy of scale - physical, marketing, risk-bearing, financial and administrative
- Highly repetitive tasks can lead to mischief on the production lines

and this represents a diseconomy of scale

- Types of corporate growth - vertical, lateral and horizontal
- Reasons for corporate growth - economies of scale, product differentiation and market dominance

The way to structure this is shown in Figure 2.

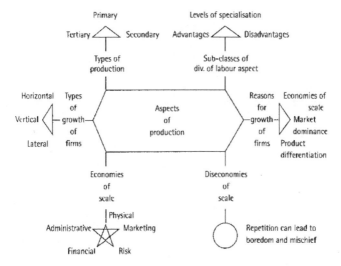

Figure 2. Example of a studygram for students of commerce

Use acronyms

OK, so the shapes help you know if you have missed any details, but they don't help you remember what all the individual items are. How do you do that?

See if you can make an acronym with the first letters of each item. You may have to juggle the letters around to do so and you can add vowels if it will help. WTRPT, for example, could be rearranged to become TPWTR which, with appropriate vowels added, becomes TAP WATER.

Suppose a law student had to memorise all the common law cases connected with a certain point of law - right to light, for example. Suppose the cases were:

Edwards v. Lambert
Andrews v. Morgan
Sanders v. Porter
Montgomery v. Smith Ellis
v. James
Norris v. Jones

Tompkins v. Handley
Hendon v. Swift

(All these cases are fictitious and used just for demonstration purposes.) Rearrange them and you could make the word EASEMENT from the initial letters. If you can recall the first names, they will act as recall cues for the second names of the cases. There is firm evidence that, where pairs are concerned, the first item of the pair acts as a cue for the recall of the second.

They won't all be this simple. You'll usually have to be a bit creative, but by juggling letters and adding vowels you will often be able to make a suitable acronym out of a list.

Use acrostics

If you can't make an acronym, then what you do is make an *acrostic*. An acrostic is a phrase each word of which starts with the initial letter of one of the things you want to remember. You may not always be able to make an acronym, but you will always be able to make an acrostic, so all the eventualities are now covered.

Suppose a management lecturer wanted his or her students to remember a list of parts of a business plan. Suppose those elements were:

- introduction
- objectives
- management
- manpower
- marketing
- strategies
- production
- legal
- finance

(No claim is made that these are the important elements of a business plan; the example is merely for demonstration purposes.)
He could tell them to remember the phrase Isle of Man money makes several people lavish fortunes.

Music teachers have for long used both the acronym and acrostic methods to teach their pupils the notes of the scale: F, A, C and E (the notes in the spaces) make the acronym FACE; and E, G, B, D and F (the notes on the lines) make the acrostic Every Good Boy Deserves Favour.

Lists of letters are often hard to learn. That is one of the reasons some children have trouble with spelling. However, if you use all the letters to make a phrase, the spelling of a difficult word is often mastered instantaneously, never to be forgotten. Take the word *because,* for example. This causes problems for many young children, but if they remember the phrase Big Elephants Can Always Upset Small Elephants, the difficulty disappears immediately. Later we will deal with how the *Five x Five System* helps with spelling in more detail.

To summarise
So, to recap, on the sub-principles of the chunking principle, use:
* chunking
* hierarchies
* shapes
* acronyms
* acrostics

Time to test your skills
OK, let's have a little test of your skill development.
1. Take a list of 40 names, picked more or less randomly from the telephone directory. Use the whole book, not just a section, and just close your eyes and open a page where your whim takes you. Learn the list for four minutes and then test yourself.
2. Take another list of 40 names picked in the same way and group them according to their initial letters. Draw one of the studygram shapes around each group. Make an acronym or an acrostic for each one. Don't even try to rehearse them. Test yourself after four minutes.

Which was most successful, the learned list, or the worked list?

2

Using Associations

The second principle of the *Five x Five System* is *image formation* and the five sub-principles you must learn are these:

- make your images positive
- use both sides of your brain
- use all your senses
- make your images interesting
- use rhyme and rhythm

It is now well established that most of the storage in long-term memory involves association — one thing being associated with another. A very quick and effective way to achieve storage is to deliberately associate what you want to store with an image. An added advantage is that while much of what you will want to store will be largely left-hemisphere material, e.g. names of things, descriptions, details of process etc., visual images are produced and stored in the right hemisphere. When you associate something, expressed in language, with a visual image, you are making an association across the two different hemispheres of the brain. This is very powerful when it comes to recall.

The connections can be obvious — it's quicker that way, but they don't have to be. In fact, research shows that the more novel, creative and subtle connections work best. This is because there is more thought involved and the more thought, the more neural roots are laid down. The more of these there are, the more likely it is that your focal attention will find a path to the material you want to retrieve.

We now know what makes a particularly effective mnemonic image and these qualities form the sub-principles of this part of the system.

Positive images work best
For most people, positive images work best. In fact, if images are
highly negative our minds may block them from conscious recall.

Use both sides of the brain
Each side of the brain functions in a different way. The left
hemisphere handles sequential stuff like time, language, logic and
so on; the right hemisphere handles static, spatial things like
emotions, feelings, shapes, position, distance, size and form. If you
seek to memorise a speech or poem purely by rehearsal of the
words, you'll be limiting your memory potential very severely -
cutting it almost by half. To use both sides of the brain you need to
visualise the images that relate to the words of your speech or
poem. Feel the feelings and the emotions involved. This is highly
important if you are an actor learning your lines.
    Another advantage of taking a consciously bi-hemispherical
approach to learning is that right-brain storage offers random access.
This differs from left-brain storage, where you have to chug through
the chains of material to get to the bits you want to retrieve.
Things work the other way round too. Suppose an electronics
engineering student was trying to commit a circuit board to memory.
He or she could add a powerful left-brain dimension to the storage
by counting the number of resistors, capacitors, switches and
transistors. He could count the number of sub-routines and visualise
the route of an electrical current with various controls activated in
the circuit. When something in a spatial system evades recall, it is
often because some other item in long-term memory is getting in the
way (see Chapter 5). The left hemisphere, sequential storage will
provide a roundabout route to the material.

Use all your senses
The third sub-principle is *use all your senses:*

- sight
- sound
- smell
- touch
- taste

The various kinds of sensory data are stored in different sites of the
brain. There are even different sites for different aspects of a single
sense. For example, where visual data is concerned, shape, size,
movement, position and colour are all stored in different places.

The mind does not seem to distinguish between images formed in the imagination and images perceived in the real world when it comes to storage. In fact, imagined ones work better, because you can elaborate them and endow them with all the qualities that make them mnemonically effective.

The more senses that are involved, the more neural roots that will be laid down, and so the more likely your focal attention will find a path to the material you are seeking to retrieve.

Sight

For most people, sight is the obvious first sense to use. Suppose you were seeking to commit to memory the name Janet Hunter. You might visualise her as a hunter of gannets, a gannet hunter. Just for an instant, see her in your mind's eye, creeping up on the birds with a spear in her hand. Such creativity may not come naturally to those who have been used to the discipline of left-hemisphere dominated thinking. However, with a little practice the skill will become increasingly easy and your ready wit will develop so that appropriate images will spring quickly to mind.

Sound

Give your images a sound dimension, for in doing so you give the memory trace an extra pathway. Imagine the sound of her steps treading down the coarse grass and brittle rushes, as she creeps up on her prey. As soon as you do this, you increase your chance of recall very significantly, for your focal attention is more likely to fall upon a relevant pathway if there are two types of sense memory paths rather than just one. Sound aspects and visual aspects are stored in very different regions of the brain.

Touch

Add a tactile dimension. Imagine you are there on the hunt with her and you tap her arm to alert her attention to something. Feel the heat of the soft flesh. Tactile sense data is stored in the somatosensory cortex. Adding this dimension lays down yet another pathway.

Taste

Now add a taste dimension. Imagine her putting her hand over your mouth to stop you speaking and frightening away the prey. Taste the salty sweat from her hand on your lips.

Smell

The sense of smell is extremely useful in memory recall. It brings to mind large amounts of detail from autobiographical memory. A single whiff of something can immediately transport your imagination to a time in the distant past and reveal to you a long-forgotten experience in great detail. A special feature of the olfactory sense is that smell data goes straight from the sense organs to the olfactory cortex of the brain, unlike other kinds of sense data which go to an intermediate relay station known as the *thalamus,* before they reach their special processing centres in the cerebral cortex.

The reason for this is probably that smell was once our most important sense, as is the case with other animals. It isn't any longer, but our evolution has not yet caught up.

You may find it a little difficult to conjure up a smell aspect to your image, but with a little practice this ability will improve. It doesn't have to be profound to add a meaningful extra trace.

Make your images interesting

The fourth sub-principle of the *Five x Five System* is *make your images interesting.* There are a number of well-proven ways in which you can do that and they are provided below. Make them:

- colourful
- moving
- humorous
- exaggerated

Make your images colourful

You're on the tube train. Opposite you is a row of people dressed in greens, browns and greys - all except one. That person is dressed in yellow trousers, a bright red shirt, and has blue hair. Who will you remember?

As you walk up the drive to your door there are birds hopping around in the garden - sparrows and a lone chaffinch. If asked about the birds in the garden later, which would you most readily recall? The chaffinch, of course. You may well have not even noticed the sparrows. That is part of the reason you remember coloured things more easily - because they grab your attention in the first place. In fact, nature has made the sparrows dull so that they will not be so easily noticed by predators.

It's not only the attentional aspect that makes colours important in memory terms, however. Colour is processed in a special area of the brain and, therefore, another retrieval pathway or set of pathways is laid down.

Make your images move

Moving images grasp the attention. If things don't move we soon fail to see them. This is why some animals remain perfectly still if a predator is about. They trust it will not notice them if they keep still. We habituate quickly to non-moving stimuli. Soldiers use this means to avoid being spotted. If an enemy is present, they freeze their movement and lie still until the threat has gone.

Movement has its own special areas of the brain. Some aspects are processed in an area known as V3, but area V4 is devoted to the processing of movement. If this is damaged, patients cannot perceive movement at all. Their world is perfectly still. It's hard to imagine, isn't it? The V prefixes of these areas simply stand for *visual cortex.*

So there are two good reasons why we remember moving things better. Firstly, we attend to them more in the first place. Secondly, extra processing in the visual areas of the brain lays down extra pathways.

Make your images humorous

Funny things are remembered well. This is because humour is positive and most of us remember positive things better than negative ones. Another reason is that humorous events often do not make complete sense. They contain absurdities and contradictions. They often require us to relax the boundaries of our sense of reality. Our minds have to do a bit of work to accommodate them and the more processing involved, the deeper the memory trace will be. Incomplete things are remembered better than complete things. Fishermen always remember the one that got away, and no love lingers in the heart like that which is unrequited or out of reach.

Exaggerate your images

Which would you remember most, the smell of a daisy or a rose? The smell of a garden or that of a farmyard? I have little doubt you will answer the rose and the farmyard, because they are stronger smells. Which would you remember most, a handshake that was very firm, or one that was about average? The very firm handshake, I'm sure. This is because we tend to remember extreme levels better than normal levels. This may be largely because a clear comparison between the normal level and the current level can be made. The comparison causes an association of the two to be stored. Also, the perception of something outside your stored norm requires work on both the internal schema and the perception of the object, to fit it into the schema. These two processes are called accommodation (modification of the internal schema) and assimilation (distortion of the perception). The more processing that is done, the more roots are laid down and the more pathways there are to offer rapid recall. So the message is, exaggerate every quality of your image:

- if it is large, make it larger
- if it is bright, make it brighter
- if it smells, make it smell even stronger
- if it is heavy, make it even heavier
- if it makes a noise, make it louder
- if it moves, make it move faster and further
- if it is funny, make it even funnier

State the association in rhyme and rhythm
Making the association you are storing rhyme makes it particularly retrievable. This is why words of wisdom in non-literate societies were encapsulated into adages or proverbs:

> *A stitch in time,*
> *Saves nine.*

> *Red sky at night,*
> *Shepherds' delight.*
> *Red sky in the morning,*
> *Shepherds' warning.*

In ancient times paper was non-existent and parchment scarce and expensive. Consequently, stories had to be passed around and handed down orally. Rhyme provided the means of enabling people to remember them.

The reason why rhyme aids recall is partly that an extra kind of processing is required. Another reason is that rhyme is positive and pleasant to read. Even sad words are beautiful if read with rhyme. Keats's 'Ode to Melancholy' is a prime example. What could be more negative than the subject of melancholy, but the poem is a joy to read.

> *Aye, 'tis in the very temple of delight*
> *That melancholy hath her sov'reign shrine*
> *Yet seen by none, save he whose strenuous tongue*

> *Can burst joy's grape against his palette fine.*
> *His soul shall see the sadness of her might*
> *And be among her many, cloudy trophies hung.*

Here's another example of a sad poem that is a joy to read, from 'Remembrance' by Emily Bronte.

> *Cold in the grave, and the deep snow piled upon thee.*
> *Far, far removed, cold in the dreary grave! Have*
> *I forgot, my only Love, to love thee; Severed at*
> *last, by Time's all-severing wave!*
> *Cold in the earth, and fifteen wild Decembers, From*
> *those brown hills have melted into spring. Faithful,*
> *indeed, is the spirit that remembers, After such years*
> *of change and suffering.*

Could any reasonable person ever say these words, though sad, are not beautiful?

So the important message here is, state the association you have formulated in rhyme and rhythm. Even if you cannot make it rhyme, at least give it strong rhythm — make a *rap* out of it, for example:

> *Jilly Hooper*
> *Rides a scooter.*

Now let's look at these sub-principles in action, in practical everyday memory tasks.

Forming images for numbers
Three principal ways of forming images for numbers are:

- number-rhyme method
- number-shape method
- number-letter matching

Number-rhyme method
The number-rhyme method is probably the most widely used of all the methods. Any rhyming image will do, but here is a vocabulary that works very well:

- 1 is a bun
- 2 is a shoe

- 3 is a tree
- 4 is a door
- 5 is a hive
- 6 is sticks
- 7 is heaven
- 8 is a gate
- 9 is wine

Number-shape method

Some people will take to the number-shape method best, particularly if they have a relatively more spatial manner of thinking. All the numbers from 0 to 9 resemble a letter - with a bit of manipulation in some cases. Turn the number 2 ninety degrees to the left and you have a letter N. Take the first word you find in the dictionary that begins with the letter N and that is your image for the number 2. You ignore the second consonant, because you don't get many words with only one, but the word selected for a single digit should have no more than two consonants (H's W's and Y's excluded). In my dictionary the word is NAG. Think of a horse. Exaggerate it. Make it an old nag. Hear it snort and stamp. Smell its sweaty, horsy smell. Feel its coarse coat.

Let's look at another example. Which letter does a number 5 look like? It's like an S. Select the first word in the dictionary that begins with S and has no more than two other consonants. SAIL will do. It doesn't have to be the very first one in the dictionary, if that doesn't make a clear image. The *Five x Five System, Number-Shape Vocabulary* is given below:

Number	Letter		Image
0	O	The resemblance between the number 0 and the letter O is obvious	Owl
1	I	The resemblance between the number 1 and the letter L is obvious	Lady
2	N	Turn number 2 ninety degrees clockwise and it becomes a letter N	Nag (old horse)
3	M	Turn number 3 ninety degrees clockwise and it becomes a letter M	Mag (magazine)
4	R	Round off the corners and tilt it to the left and the letter R looks like 4	Ram
5	S	The resemblance between 5 and the letter S is obvious	Sail
6	B	The resemblance between 6 and the letter b is obvious	Bin
7	7	The letter t in brushscript font is 7	Tan
8	F	A longhand form of this letter looks rather like an 8	Fan
9	P	The resemblance between 9 and the letter p is obvious	Page (e.g. page-boy)

An advantage of this system is you can use it for multi-digit numbers. You can string several digits together into a single image. You cannot do this with the number-rhyme method. All you do is find words with more consonants, always ignoring the last one on the right in any word. In fact, to make things easy for you, 100 images for numbers are provided in Appendix 3.

Only the first three consonants in any word are used. Words to represent three-digit numbers have to have four consonants, as the rule is to ignore the last one. Numbers of more than four digits are represented by linking two or more images together. Double consonants, e.g. double ll or cc count as single letters.

Number-letter matching method

A third way of forming images for numbers is the number-letter matching method. You select a word that starts with the corresponding letter of the alphabet. For example:

- 1 = A
- 2 = B
- 3 = C and so on

The digit 2 may be expressed as the word *Bag,* because B is the second letter of the alphabet and bag is a word beginning with B that springs readily to mind. The digit 4 might be represented by the word *Daffodil,* because D is the fourth letter of the alphabet and daffodil is a word beginning with that letter that immediately springs to mind. It is a good image to use, because it has colour and a distinctive smell to reinforce it.

You can use compound words or forename-surname combinations for two-digit numbers. For example:

- 28 = Bee-hive
- 44 = Donald Duck

This method has greater capacity than the number-rhyme method, which can only handle single digits, but its capacity is not as great as the number-shape method, which can handle three-digit numbers in a single image.

To summarise

To sum up what we have said in this chapter, the second principle of the *Five x Five System* is form images and the five sub-principles are:
- make images positive
- use both sides of the brain
- use all your senses
- make your images interesting
- give them rhyme and rhythm

Time to test your skills

Take 20 names from the telephone directory. Form images for them (you can invent what they look like) and test your recall immediately afterwards.

- Generate 20 numbers more or less randomly and form images for them. When you have done so, test your recall of the entire list.

- Select 20 words from an English/foreign language dictionary and form images to connect their sounds with their meanings in English. When you have done so, test your recall of the words and their meanings.

3

Chaining

The third principle of the *Five x Five System* is chaining and there are five sub-principles. Each provides an alternative means of doing this. They are:

- story method
- poem method
- picture method
- room method
- loci method

Story method
The story method involves linking the images together into a story. It doesn't have to make perfect sense; it only has to have grammar - sentences made of subject, object, verb and, perhaps, complement. That's enough to make them memorable.

Suppose you had to memorise a lot of names. Suppose they were:

- Page
- Smith
- Ray
- Parker
- Harris
- Thurston

- Barker
- Swan
- Cantor
- Storey
- Carson
- Wood

You will have already formed images for each at stage 2 of the process. Now you need to chain them together. In fact, you may start this process at the same time as image formation — chaining them as you go. Your story might be as follows.

The (black) **Smith, Page(d) Carson** (think of the famous jockey, Willie Carson) who **Cantor(ed)** over to the **Wood.** He could see a **Ray** of sunlight high in the trees. **Harris,** dressed in tweed, had already **Parker(d)** and was telling a **Stor(e)y** to a **Swan** that was quenching its **Thurst(on),** while the dog Bark(er)ed at it.

It doesn't have to make complete sense. Nor do the names to be remembered have to match completely the terms in the story. A vague connection should be enough to jog your memory.

Poem method

The second way of chaining is the poem method. This has been well proven to be an effective memory aid. In fact, oral cultures have used it for centuries for passing down the wisdom of the culture. We still have some of it in poetic form today:

> *Red sky at night*
> *Shepherds delight*
> *Red sky in the morning*
> *Shepherds warning*

The classical epics were told in rhyme and regular metre and still exist in this form today, albeit now on paper.

There are two ways to make your mnemonic poems. One method is to distort words to make them rhyme as you go. The other way is to make totally sensible statements and give them rhyme and rhythm by adding words, rather than distorting them.

Making the stories first

A simple way is to construct the stories first and then tweak them into verse afterwards. Here is an example. Take the same list of names and construct a story with them. You could tweak it into verse like this:

> The **Smith Paged Carson**
> Who **Cantor(ed) to the Wood(s) on Parker** Where
> **Harris** was telling a **Stor(e)y** to a **Swan who**
> **Ra(y)ced** to the river, to quench his **Thurst(on)** with
> **Barker.**

A few of the words have changed position and some of the names have been distorted, to make it rhyme.

The other way is to make a sensible story, with no distortion of the words, and make it rhyme simply by adding words. Example:

> **Smith** read a **Page** with **Cars on**
> And a **Wood** carved **Swan** and a **Parker** pen
> **Storey** and **Harris** in his tweed shone
>
>   A **Ray** towards **Cantor, Thurston** and **Barker's** men.

This has both rhyme and rhythm. All that was necessary was a bit of rearrangement of the order and the addition of a few rhyming words. When the list is long it is likely that opportunities for rhyme and rhythm will present themselves.

Picture method

An alternative way of forming chains between images is to build them into a picture. Each picture tells a story and the more complex it is, the bigger the story. When your chains of images are stored in a picture, you just scan from top left to bottom right, noting each image and recalling the material it represents. You can even make your picture dynamic - things going on, like a piece of video footage. Don't make it too long, or it simply becomes a story. Make it just long enough to give dynamic quality to the images - perhaps 30 seconds or so.

Advantages

An advantage of this kind of chaining method is that you can see the whole schema at once. Consequently, you can more or less randomly access any bit of it. You can't do this with stories or poems.

Abstract concepts cannot be directly represented in pictures, for things like luck, profit or motivation, for example, don't have a visible image, or any other sensory image, for that matter. That doesn't prevent them from featuring in a story, but it does prevent them from being directly represented in a picture. You can, however, use a symbol for the undepictable, for example, a heart for love, or a cash register for profit.

It's not so easy to show personal names in a picture either, unless you can draw brilliantly and quickly. Furthermore, if you are committing lots of bibliographical details such as law cases to memory, you won't know what the named people look like anyway. What you have to do is distort the names, so that they do suggest an image. The name *Greenspan,* for example, could be depicted as a green bridge, and the name *Penfield* could be represented by a field where pens are growing. The name *Schopenhaur* could be depicted as a regular, one-hour TV slot, one in which people showed their unusual pens - *Show Pen Hour.* The name *Loftus* could be depicted as a loft ladder.

This kind of chaining method will suit some people more than others; those with a more spatial thinking style are the most likely to favour it. However, even the most left-brain dominant people will benefit from deliberate right-brain processing. If you have the time to construct both a relatively left-brain schema (e.g. a story or a poem) and a relatively right-brain one (a picture), you will more or less double your memory traces and more than double your likelihood of recall. Not only are there more recall paths, but each schema will contain cues to its counterpart.

Room method

The room method was first used by the Romans. What you do is keep an image of a room in your head. It should contain only a few features, for example, a table, a dining chair, an armchair, a settee, telephone on a shelf, a vase on a window sill, a piano and stool, an electric fire, a radiator, a TV and a radio. When you have a list of things you want to commit to memory, you mentally place each one on a different item of furniture. Then, when you need to recall them, think of the room and what is placed on each feature. Here is an example. Suppose in your personal memory room you have the features/items listed above. Suppose you want to remember to:

- Call at your friend's house to deliver a birthday card
- Go to the bank
- Go to the dentist
- Go to the butcher's
- Take a coat to the cleaner's
- Call at the shoe repairer's to see if your shoes are ready
- Buy some black cotton
- Buy a local *Advertiser* paper
- Book a theatre ticket.

You could call to mind your personal room and mentally place:

- Your friend's birthday card on the table
- Your cheque book on the dining chair
- Your dentist in the armchair
- Some fresh meat on the settee. Think of the mess it is making.
- Your coat over the telephone. Hear the muffled ring. You might imagine you've placed it there for that purpose.
- Your shoes in the vase on the window sill
- A cotton reel on the keys of the piano
- The *Advertiser* paper on the piano stool
- A theatre ticket on the top of the electric fire. (See it beginning to curl from the heat.)

Advantages

The main merits of the room system are its simplicity and its flexibility. You keep the same room in your head and use it over and over again. You don't have to keep setting up new rooms ones.

Disadvantages
A drawback of this method is that it has very limited capacity. To be manageable, your room can only contain a few items of furniture and that means it offers only a small number of pegs for memory material. Another disadvantage is that it is susceptible to proactive interference. Material you hang on the various pegs may be contaminated, and even replaced, by material which was previously hung on them.

The Greek method of loci
The Greek method of loci is the oldest known method of chaining. It was used by ancient Greek travelling lecturers, known as the sophists, to memorise their lectures. They would walk around public buildings and commit their layout to memory. Using a different building for each lecture, they would mentally lay each main point in a different loom. When they gave a lecture they would mentally walk around the appropriate building, recalling each main point as they went.

Advantages
This method has an unlimited storage capacity. The more you have to memorise, the bigger the building you find. Office blocks contain an enormous number of loci for memory purposes. You don't have to use buildings either. You can use gardens, factory or school sites, farmyards, housing estates, villages, towns or cities. A second advantage is that, because you use different buildings or sites for different memory tasks, you don't have to keep erasing material.
It doesn't have the instant access qualities that the picture method has, but the advantages it does offer make it the most powerful method of all for memorising. For memorising lectures and any other task requiring sequential recall, it is ideal.

To summarise
- The story method is simple. Stories only need to make rough sense and this can be achieved by adding or distorting words.
- The poem method is a well-proven technique. Make stories first, then give them rhyme and rhythm.
- The picture method offers random access. It also adds a spatial dimension to the otherwise predominantly sequential storage resulting from the use of other chaining methods.
- The room method is simple and durable.

- The method of loci provides unlimited capacity and permanent storage.

Time to test yourself

Select 20 names, more or less randomly, from your telephone directory. Memorise them using the story method. Switch your attention away from the subject by doing something else for ten minutes. Test yourself again.

- Select another 20 names and do the same using the poem method.
- Select another 20 names and do the same using the picture method.
- Select another 20 names and do the same using the room method.
- Select another 20 names and do the same using the Greek method of loci.

Which one seems to work best for you?

4

Enhancing Consolidation

The fourth principle of the *Five x Five System* is enhancing consolidation. The five sub-principles are as follows:

■ rehearse by repetition
■ where lists are concerned, learn middles, then ends, and then beginnings
■ direct your memorising efforts with the stages of vulnerability in mind
■ minimise retroactive interference
■ use consolidation-enhancing substances safely

Even the most effectively stored memories remain vulnerable for a while. Initial storage has to be consolidated and this is not part of the same process as initial storage. Indeed, consolidation may involve several processes at different stages. What we know about the consolidation phase makes it possible to create memory-enhancement techniques that are appropriate at each step of the way. They range from repetition in the early stage to compensating for the serial reproduction effect and even selecting memorising periods to optimise their effectiveness. This chapter will show you how to get the best out of this stage of the memorising process.

Extending sensory memory and short-term memory

When information comes in via the senses, it is first stored in sensory memory. This only lasts about two seconds, but we can extend that time by rehearsal. When someone tells you their name, for example, repeat it to yourself several times. By doing this you are restarting the clock over and over again. The longer the material stays in sensory memory, the more chance it has of entering short-term memory. You can do this with all kinds of information — names, numbers, dates and so on. Stress the rhythm and rhyme, where present, as well as the sound. This will make it more memorable.

You will recall that in the first chapter you learned how to prepare telephone numbers for entry into short-term memory by chunking the six or seven-bit number into just two bits of data. I he lesson now is to repeat these two bits to yourself, to give your short-term memory more time to accept the material.

Overcoming the serial reproduction effect

Have you noticed that when you try to memorise a song, a poem or speech, the first line sticks easily enough, but the rest doesn't. Recall is affected by what is known as the *serial reproduction effect*. This refers to the fact that we tend to naturally remember more from the beginning of a list than the end, and least of all rum the middle portion. It applies to any information in serial form, for example, stories, poems, songs, lists, long numbers and card sequences.

The tendency to recall best from the beginning of a series is known as the *primacy effect*. The fact that the end portion is easier to remember than the middle is known as the *recency effect*. It happens like this because rehearsal is most practicable in respect of the early part of the series and the memory trace of the last part has had less time to decay than the rest. It will also have been less subject to retroactive interference, as there were fewer similar items following it into the working memory than was the case in respect of the middle portion. The way to overcome the serial reproduction effect is simply to learn the middle bit first, then the end portion, and then the beginning. You are then making the most vulnerable bit the strongest and the second most vulnerable bit stronger than the first portion (the naturally strongest bit). You are then standing the serial reproduction effect on its head.

Getting through the vulnerable periods

The type of vulnerability that affects declarative memory changes over time. In the sensory memory stage it's dependent on the echo remaining long enough for the short-term memory process to find a pattern-match in another part of memory. Once it finds a match, it takes the material in. This two minute-long process can be extended by repetition of the material.

It must be recoded semantically, though, within fifteen to thirty seconds of entering short-term memory, otherwise the trace will be lost. This fifteen to thirty seconds can also be extended by repetition of the material.

Once you've worked semantically on the material, e.g. associated it with something else in your memory, it passes to long-term memory.

It is even vulnerable there for a while. You need to reinforce it, particularly after about an hour. This is, in fact, why teachers and lecturers should always sum up at the end of a lesson.

Another vulnerable stage occurs at around five hours from initial storage. You would be wise, therefore, to reinforce storage at around that time by testing and correcting errors and omissions in your recall. Following this, the material should be reinforced at the end of a day, after the first week, and after the first month. This is known as the day/week/month method. It is a very powerful means of reinforcing memory.

Minimising interference

The main cause of forgetting is interference from other material in memory. It may be material stored prior to the material you are Trying to recall, or it may have been stored after it. Interference from previously stored information is known as *proactive interference,* because its effect is forward acting. Interference from material stored after what it is you are seeking to recall is known as *retroactive interference,* because it has a backward effect.

Proactive interference increases throughout life, because we have an increasing store of material to get in the way. This is why older people are more forgetful than younger people.

You can't really do anything to significantly reduce this kind of interference. You can memorise first thing in the morning, when you have not stored anything for seven or eight hours, but there is a lifetime of storage prior to the moment you went to sleep and that too can get in the way.

In addition, the earlier in the day you memorise things, the more retroactive interference there will be from the rest of the day. On the other hand, if you memorise too late in the day, you won't be able to reinforce it at the one-hour and five-hour intervals. The best balance might be between late morning and late afternoon.

While you can't stop the proactive kind of interference, you can prevent the retroactive kind undermining consolidation. If you run over the material you have stored and reinforced earlier in the day just before going to sleep, you will have a good chance of seven or eight hours of freedom from retroactive interference while consolidation takes place.

I reiterate, though, this is a quick run through what we are talking about. Just before bed is not the best time to do the initial memorising job, or the one-hour or five-hour consolidation procedures. You are likely to be tired for one thing and concentrated mental effort will keep you awake. The best thing to do is carry out those procedures earlier in the day and just run over the material, which by then you will easily recall, just before going to sleep.

Memory drugs

There are substances that aid memory consolidation. Some are double-edged swords, being so harmful in other ways that any beneficial effect on memory consolidation is outweighed by the health hazards they cause. Nicotine is a prime example. While it aids consolidation, it is highly dangerous to health and, in fact, in the end can lead to *multiple-infarct* syndrome (haemorrhaging or clotting in the brain). This, itself, will have very damaging effects on memory.

A substance that has a positive effect on memory consolidation and which, in moderation, is more or less harmless, is caffeine in both tea and coffee. A further advantage is that it helps keep you alert while you are memorising.

There are other substances, known as smart drugs, which claim to have a good effect on memory. These include:

- DHEA
- Hydergene
- Choline
- Ginkgo biloba extract

To summarise

- Repeat new material silently several times.
- Overcome the serial reproduction effect by learning ends, then middles, and then beginnings.
- Use the day/week/month method to reinforce storage.
- Test yourself on stored material just before going to sleep.
- Drink tea or coffee when memorising.

Time to test your skills

List the first 40 nouns (people, places or things) you find in your dictionary. Spend four minutes memorising the list, working from beginning to end. Test yourself after a delay of ten minutes.

List the next 40 nouns in the dictionary. Spend one minute memorising roughly the middle one-third section. Then spend one minute memorising roughly the last one-third portion. Lastly, spend the last two minutes memorising the entire list from start to finish. Test yourself after a delay of ten minutes.

Which list did you remember best?

List the next 40 nouns in your dictionary. Memorise them early
in the day and certainly before the end of the afternoon. Test yourself
at around 9 p.m.

List the next 40 nouns and memorise them about the same time of
the day. Then test and correct yourself after an hour, overlearning
wherever there were errors and omissions. Test and correct yourself
again after five hours (again overlearning as necessary). Test yourself
at around 9 p.m.

Which list did you recall best?

List the next 40 nouns from your dictionary. Memorise them in the
early evening and then forget about them until the next morning. Test
your recall.

List the next 40 nouns from your dictionary and memorise them
early in the evening. Test yourself and correct for any errors and
omissions just before you go to sleep. Test yourself the next morning.

Which list did you recall best?

5

Overcoming Forgetting

The fifth principle of the *Five x Five System* is overcoming forgetting and the five sub-principles are:

- using the tip of the tongue technique
- backtracking
- using cues
- inducing relaxation
- reconstructing

You have learned how to store and consolidate effectively but, ironically, that doesn't automatically mean you'll be able to retrieve what you have stored. This is because retrieval is a different process. Hut if you haven't stored and consolidated effectively, there will be nothing there for it to retrieve, so you have first got to learn to More and consolidate well. Assuming you have done so, this chapter will show you how to maximise your retrieval ability.

Using the tip of the tongue technique
How often have you said, 'Oh, it's on the tip of my tongue', when you have been trying to recall a name or a word? This is more than just a figure of speech; it's quite close to the physical truth. When we hear a name, we sub vocally say it to ourselves and this involves minute mouth movements and the associated neural processes. We
then store the psychomotor process along with the name and the two become associated. Recall one side of the pair and the other side is likely to arrive in your consciousness. So let your mouth and your tongue take the lead in the recall process. Try making different initial letter sounds, then different first syllable sounds. Try combinations of syllables. Say it silently if you're with other people. Try different:

- initial letters
- first syllables
- syllable counts
- second and third syllables
- syllable stress patterns

You will usually know when you are close on any of these trials.

Backtracking

The autobiographical part of our long-term memory contains a continuous and connected record of our experiences. Some aspects of that experience will not have been attended to sufficiently to get into long-term memory, but other aspects will have, so there will be connections. Because we conduct our lives intelligently, there will be a retraceable route along which you can backtrack to an earlier time, even though it may not be entirely direct. If there are gaps, you can leap them by turning your attention to the context - the setting, the people there at the time, what they were talking about, and so on. Your implicit memory will have been storing these details in association with other aspects of the experience, including what it is you are seeking to recall. Backtracking is a good technique for recovering otherwise unyielding memories, because the recall difficulty is often due to an obstruction in the pathway to consciousness. Backtracking can find an indirect route that will go around the obstacle.

Using cues

The most common cause of forgetting is something getting in the way, obstructing the path from long-term memory to consciousness. What you need is, metaphorically speaking, a 'reflection in a mirror' to see around the obstacle. Fortunately, our implicit memory stores aspects of the context and these serve this purpose. Peripheral details, like aspects of environment, the people present, the sounds, the conditions, and even things like your mood are stored in the memory in association with the material you are seeking to recall. Shift your focus from the direct path on to one of these other aspects and you will usually find that the material you are seeking to recall, obscured in the direct path but not in this indirect one, springs immediately into consciousness.

External and internal cues

External cues are the aspects of the physical environment in which the material was stored. Internal cues are things like feelings, moods and thoughts.

Building cues in deliberately
These implicit memory cues are stored automatically, but we can enhance the process by consciously making associations between what we want to remember, on the one hand, and various aspects of our environment, our mood, our thoughts and so on, on the other.

Leaving the implicit and reflex memory to store the associations automatically results in building cues into the *storage context* (the situation in which the material was stored). If you take conscious control of part of this process, you can build cues into the *recall context* too (the context in which you are likely to have to recall the material, e.g. the exam room). This is a very powerful recall strategy.

Inducing relaxation
Two things that impair recall ability are stress and anxiety. When these prevent recall the more you struggle with the task, the more frustrated and anxious you become. It's even worse if you feel you ought to be able to recall it. Forgetting becomes a self-generating process, because the frustration and anxiety, which derives from your inability to recall what you feel you ought to have been able to recall, itself takes up some of the channel capacity and so restricts the memory process further. The way to avoid this is to quickly induce relaxation.

Relaxing in five stages
It is easy to induce relaxation. Working up from your feet to your head, you tightly clench the muscles of each limb for a count of ten and then let go. Use controlled breathing - instead of expanding your chest as you breathe in, inflate your stomach. Deflate it as you breathe out. Try it for yourself, using the exercises listed below.

Relaxing your feet
Clench the muscles of your feet. Count slowly to ten and then relax them. Take ten slow, deep breaths, while you focus on the relaxation in your feet.

Relaxing your legs
Clench all the muscles in your legs. Count to ten and let go. Take ten slow, deep breaths.

Relaxing your torso
Tightly clench all the muscles of which you are aware in your torso. Count slowly to ten and then let go. Take ten slow, deep breaths as you focus on the relaxation in your torso.

Relaxing your arms

Tightly contract all your arm muscles and count slowly to ten. Relax them and take ten slow, controlled breaths as you feel the relaxation in your arms.

Relaxing your face and neck

Clench every muscle of which you are aware in your face and neck. Count slowly to ten and let go. Focus on the relaxation that results.

Patching the gaps

Often people are unwilling to consciously make estimates or guesses about what they have stored in their memory. However, some degree of reconstruction is a natural part of the recall process.

Not all autobiographical recall is guesswork and reconstruction. Some bits are accurate, but the bits in between them are reconstructions or guesses, for we don't actually recall experiences in their entirety. We remember bits and we patch the gaps with material from thoughts, conversations, stories, dreams, rumours, what we have read in the papers, what seems to fit the gaps, and so on.

When we recall experiences from memory, we distort them to fit our present frame of reference. Frames of reference change over time and so recalled memories too will change. When we recall and distort memories, we then re-store the distorted form, so that even what is buried in our long-term memory becomes distorted.

Furthermore, what you might assume is a guess will not be as random as you think. I would argue that pure guessing, in the sense of generating a purely random response, is actually beyond the capability of the human mind. The mind generates ideas in a connective way, each one being dependent on its predecessor in consciousness, and on schemata (knowledge structures laid down by experience) that relate to the initial thought. As Freud pointed out, nothing that occurs in the mind does so fortuitously. When you understand these things you will not be so reluctant to consciously reconstruct.

To summarise

- Use the tip of the tongue technique for difficulty in recalling names, words and short numbers with which you usually have no problem.
- Backtrack to get around memory blocks.
- Cues are automatically installed, but can be enhanced consciously.

- Relax — struggling to recall something is often counter-productive.
- Reconstruction is permissible and natural.

Time to test your skill

Memorise the names of 20 people whose photos you find in a newspaper. Spend five minutes doing so and then test yourself after 20 minutes, using the tip of the tongue technique where necessary. Take a random list of 20 digits and memorise them, using the story method of chaining. Test yourself after five minutes, using backtracking where necessary.

Take a page of text and memorise it, deliberately building cues into features of the room in which you're sitting. Test your recall after five minutes.

Part 2
Putting the
Five x Five System
Into practice

Having concentrated on the principles of the *Five x Five System* so far, we are now going to shift our focus and take a more practical approach, focusing on handling particular memory problems.

6

Remembering Names and Faces

If you want to improve your ability to put names to faces, this is how to use the principles of the *Five x Five* System to do so.

Association
The best kind of association to make is one that relates the person's attributes to their name. Sometimes the appropriate association is glaringly obvious:

- Mrs. Waitrose has a great nose.
- Mr. Tate could lose some weight.
- Mrs. Quinn is rather thin.

Sometimes it is non-physical attributes that most readily suggest a rhyming association. For example:

- Mr. Palmer is a farmer.
- Mrs. Window is always at the window.
- Mrs. Flowers has a garden full of flowers.

These are the exceptions, though, and a method is needed that will apply to all cases.

You are at an advantage if you know what names mean and it isn't difficult to learn the meanings of common names. If you know what a name means, you immediately have something tangible with which to make the association. Furthermore, you have a source of preliminary chatter of the kind that will flatter the person to whom you are talking:

Andrew. That means warrior, doesn't it?'
Everybody loves to hear the sound of their own name and this gives you the opportunity to set off on the right foot. First impressions are the deepest and you will be off to a good start if you show interest in their name.

It will also cause you to repeat the name several times. This keeps restarting the clocks of sensory memory and short-term memory, to give you more time for the name to enter your long-term memory.

Comment on both names. Your knowledge will impress and interest them, as well as flattering them. While you are discussing the name, you can observe them closely and make preliminary lodgments about their inner state. Ask about their life, where they come from, what they do for a living, their family background, their life experience, their likes and dislikes, and all the time relating the knowledge acquired to their facial features and to their names. How much is their experience and background reflected in their face - their expression, the lines and quality of their skin, the leanness of their cheeks, or otherwise? Faces are media upon which all life experience is written. You only have to look for it. Any association between their attributes and their name, however, is likely to be fortuitous, but it can still be interesting and certainly beneficial for memory purposes.

Lists of some of the most common forenames and surnames, together with their meanings, are provided at the end of this book. Learn them well and use them when you are storing people's names.

Remember, when you are making name-face associations, make them positive, use both left-brain and right-brain processing and use all the senses. Make the connections interesting and sum them up in short, rhythmical rhyme.

Enhancing consolidation

The most vulnerable time of all for storage of your name-face associations is the first few seconds. How often have you been told someone's name, only to forget it more or less immediately? This happens because when you meet someone for the first time you have a large amount of diverse data trying to get into your perceptual set: the name, the face, the expression, the eye contact, the feel of the handshake, the quality of the clothes, and more; and that's only the personal data.

There is all the situational data too: the sounds around you, the person who introduced you, the setting, and so on. Then there is all the data from your own body. You may be aware of shyness, nervousness or anxiety when looking into the new person's eyes. You may be experiencing positive feelings like attraction, interest, curiosity, and so on. You may be wondering what the other person is thinking about you. Masses of data are bombarding your senses, much of which can only get into your short-term memory by displacing data already there. It's no wonder names get lost in the short-term memory system.

How can you prevent it? Repetition is the answer. This is how you reinforce memory at the sensory memory and short-term memory stages. Make a point of repeating names out loud when you are told them. Then make a point of using them often in the conversation. Commenting on the meaning of the names gives an additional opportunity to repeat them. This keeps restarting the clock of sensory memory and short-term memory, giving more time for the name to enter the short-term and long-term memory stores, respectively.

Refresh your memory on all the name-face associations you've stored whenever you get a moment to yourself.

Overcoming forgetting of names

If you find you cannot quite put a name to a face, but you feel it is on the tip of your tongue, it probably is. If you use your tongue to silently make different, initial syllable sounds, you will often find that the name will suddenly present itself to you when you have made the right tongue and mouth movements. This is because your mind has stored the association between the sound of the name and the psychomotor skill involved in physically producing the sound. Recall one side of the association (physical movements) and the other side will often arrive in your consciousness too.

When you first hear a name, your implicit memory stores associations between the name and various aspects of the context surroundings, other people and activities going on etc. You are not aware of these associations; that's why this part of memory is called *implicit*. However, if you deliberately recall the data of the context in which you heard the name for the first time, you may well hit upon one side (contextual detail) of one of these associations. If you do, the other side (name) will often present itself in your conscious mind too.

Things enter your consciousness linked to other things that are already there and subsequent experiences are linked, in turn, to them. The chain of experiences is only broken when you go to sleep. Just as experiences present themselves in linked form, so they are stored in linked form. Backtracking along the links, therefore, is one way to remember those things that are evading recall. This applies to names as much as to anything else.

If you are anxious, your memory will be impaired while this state of mind persists. Anxiety takes energy and this starves the thinking and recall processes. It is also something which you consciously feel and so it takes up some of your limited perceptual set. There is, therefore, less available for the conscious recall of material in memory. So don't get uptight if you can't remember a name; it won't help. It will make the recall even more unlikely. If all else fails, you can usually get the person to state their name by pausing and uttering sounds like 'erm', at the slot in your sentence where the name should come out. Most people will fill the gap by stating their own name. 'Yes. Quite', you reply. It doesn't necessarily suggest to them that you've forgotten their name; it simply suggests that you have a lot on your mind.

7

The Five x Five System and Foreign Languages

The most effective principle, when it comes to learning foreign languages, is the *image formation principle*. Select a mother tongue (own language) word that sounds like the foreign word and associate the images that each word represents.

Examples:

> The Portuguese word for cat is *gatto*. Visualise a cat-shaped cake.
>
> The Portuguese word for cheese is *queijo*. Visualise the cheese being kept in a cage, so that the mice can't get it.

This system of learning languages by image association has been around for a while. Paul Daniels wrote a book on foreign language learning, using this method. The big weakness, however, has always been that, up to now, it has only worked for those words that lend themselves readily to image formation, e.g. nouns: Cat - *gatto*, money - *dinheiro*. But how often will you use the word cat on your Algarve holiday?

> 'Good *afternoon, senhor. Have you got a cat?'*
>
> *'Can you tell me the way to the cats' home?'*

Rarely, I should say.

My interest in the use of memory techniques for language learning was revived a few years ago when I was talking with a group of foreign language teachers. I discovered that children learn foreign languages more easily than adults. I found that the methods used to teach children tended to be different from those used to teach adults. Children tend to be taught (after the first few weeks) in 100% foreign tongue. Teach adults in this way and they give up. They keep reverting to the mother tongue to clarify things. This leads to *interference* (see page 47) and a lower level of learning in the foreign language. Adult education teachers are usually part-time and get paid only for the classes they teach. If numbers drop, classes are closed and they lose their jobs. If the lessons are difficult for kids — tough; their attendance is compulsory. If lessons are hard for adults, they quit the course. So, consequently, teachers allow them to speak in the mother tongue and the result is diminished exposure to the target language, rather than concentrated exercise in using it.

I wondered if there was a way to rapidly give them enough of a grounding in the target language, so that they could easily struggle by without recourse to the mother tongue, even if they didn't know all the words to use. The mnemonic association methods around at the time would not suffice, because they only helped with words that readily lent themselves to image formation. What was needed was a way of quickly learning the common words that appear in almost every sentence. But how do you form a visual image for words like *and, if, when, the,* and so on? I guess this was why such words were missed out of the mnemonic memory courses that had once been so popular, but had gradually lost their appeal. Well, this is where this book becomes truly innovative, for I have found a way to generate images for these words — the common words that have, to date, eluded the treatment of memory trainers.

These words would not evoke an image, so the answer was to change them for words that would. Cockney rhyming slang, or something resembling it, could act as an intermediary between the mother tongue word and the foreign word. So I acquired what is known as the Dolch List. This is a list of the 200 most commonly used words, 100 of which make up 50% of everyday speech and text. The other 100 make up a further 30% so that, together, the 200 words account for 80% of everyday speech and text. I then set about devising a complete vocabulary of rhyming slang for common words. Here it is.

Rhyming Slang for Common Words

Word	Rhyming slang	Word	Rhyming slang
a	straw and hay	of	guinea and sov.
i	pastry and pie	to	old and new
it	drill and bit	he	elbow and knee
the	carrot and pea	is	hers and his
and	singer and band	that	dog and cat
in	needle and pin	was	why and because

The words above equip you to rapidly master a quarter of all speech and text in any foreign language.

Word	Rhyming slang	Word	Rhyming slang
all	Bat and ball	They	Anchor and bay
be	Leaf and tree	you	Cow and moo
for	Window and door	at	Ball and bat
his	Bubbles and fizz	are	Lager and bar
on	Janet and John	have	Slav (Picture of a Russain in native dress).
so	Suck and blow		
with	Smith (blacksmith)		
as	Trumpet and jazz	Not	Ink and blot
but	Watchman and hut	said	Sleeper and bed
had	Lass and lad	we	Lock and key
him	Gymnast and gym	about	Cider and stout
one	Currant and bun		

When you have learned all the words up to here, you will be equipped to rapidly master one-third of all the words used in everyday speech and text in any language.

Word	Rhyming slang	Word	Rhyming slang
an	Driver and van	like	Peddle and bike
before	Bells and Egor	made	Denim and fade
call	Brickie and wall	me	Smiling with glee
come	Finger and thumb	my	Hook and eye
do	Sticky and glue	now	Curtsey and bow
from	Guy Fawkes and bomb	only	Single and lonely
with	Smith (blacksmith)	other	Expectant mother
has	Curry Madras	right	Boxer and fight

if	Bendy and stiff	some	Drustick and drum
then	Egg and hen	up	Saucer and cup
two	Nail and screw	whet	Camper and tent
well	Clangour and bell	when	Bill and Ben
what	Sailor and yacht	will	Climber and hill
which	Cricket and pitch	been	King and queen
your	Lion and roar	by	Rugby and try
back	Partridge and sack	can	Lady and fan
big	Shovel and dig	did	Box and lid
came	Cards and game	first	Tyre and burst
could	Custard and pud	go	Lamp and glow
down	Circus and clown	here	Drinker and beer
get	Fisher and net	just	Duster and dust
her	Cat and purr	look	Reader and book
into	Piebald and pinto	more	Music and score
	(picture a dappled horse)	must	Iron and rust
		new	Snooker and cue
little	Ball and skittle	old	Potter and mould
make	Baker and cake	our	Castle and tower
much	Rabbit and hutch	over	Meadow and clover
know	Shoelace and bow	she	Itch and flea
off	Pig and trough	them	Diamond and gem
or	Soldier and war	this	Cuddle and kiss
about	Ticket and tout	want	Vicar and font
see	Biscuits and tea	where	Fox and lair
their	Barber and hair	where	Smudge and blur

there	Rabbit and hare	who	Tiger and zoo

When you have learned all of the above list you will be equipped to rapidly master 50% of all the terms used in everyday speech and text in any language under the sun. Learn the next 100 and you'll increase that to 80%

Word	Rhyming slang	Word	Rhyming slang
after	Joy and laughter	once	Dumbo and dunce
am	Pork and ham	play	Night and day
away	Cause an affray	read	Planter and seed
because	Them and us (football teams)	round	Fox and hound
black	Chimney and stack	saw	Floorboard and floor
bring	Bell and ring	should	Splinter and wood
don't	Doughnut (do not)	soon	Sun and the moon
far	Barman and bar	tell	Fragrance and smell
fell	Bucket and well	thing	Aeroplane and wing
		time	Lemon and lime
fly	Neck and tie	under	Lightning and thunder
gave	Razor and shave	walk	Blackboard and chalk
going	Raking and hoeing	wish	Water and fish
green	Kidney bean	again	Wind and the rain
head	Jam and bread	anohter	Hamlet's mother
house	Trap and mouse	ask	Beer and cask
keep	Jump and leap	best	Jewels and chest
left	Stave and cleft	blue	Rabbit and stew

long	Song sheet and song	day	Labour and pay
may	Dinner and tray	eat	Dinner and meat
Mr	Brother and sister	open	Dice and throw ten
fast	Sail and mast	put	Sweep and soot
Find	Clock and wind	red	Drainpipes and ted
four	Boatman and oar	run	Habit and nun
girl	Oyster and pearl	say	Corset and stay
good	Oilskin and hood	thing	Tinkle and ping
hand	Sandbit and sand	stop	Boogie and bop
help	Seaweed and kelp	than	fellow and man
how	Ploughman and plough	think	basin and sink
know	Archer and bow	to	black and blue
let	Bookie and bet	us	talk and discuss
man	Desperate dan	white	flyer and kite
men	Buddists and zen	work	shirker and shirk
never	Brainy and clever	year	whiskey and beer
always	Fountains and sprays	every	dreamer and reverie
any	Purse and penny	father	brush and lather
bad	Flatlet or pad	five	bee and hive
bird	Direct image for this word	found	noise and sound
boy	Soldier and toy	give	wide boy and spiv
dog	Direct image for this word	got	baby and cot
home	Garden and gnome	jump	cycle and pump
last	Theatre and cast	sat	rat man and rat

live	Diver and dive	take	cod and hake
many	Spinner and jenny	these	wind and breeze
mother	Sister and brother	three	laughter and glee
next	Writer and text	tree	(direct image for this word)
own	Dog and bone	very	champagne perry
ran	Bowl and bran	why	one in the eye
room	Sonic boom	would	goosberry pud
sit	Bridle and bit		
school	Muffin the mule		

Now if you learn this easy list you will immediately take a large leap in your ability to learn any language under the sun, for the image-evoking slang words remain the same whatever language you are learning. Learn the first 100 words in this list and you only then have to learn (by association methods) a mere 100 foreign words to be able to deal with 50% of everyday speech and text. Learn the whole 200 words and you will easily be able to manage communication in the foreign language. The words in between the common words can easily be dealt with by gestures. Anyone can describe a car, a train, a drink, a telephone, cold, hot, and so on, without the use of words. It's just a matter of simple mime.

The reason I initially devised the system was to give language teachers a means of imparting enough target language words to their classes quickly and easily for them to be able to struggle by in 100% foreign tongue, without resorting to mother tongue. However, the fact is that this is the single most important development in mnemonic methods for language learning so far. Nothing could propel you forward so fast in your language learning skill as this technique. I recently demonstrated on BBC Television how a working knowledge of the Welsh language could be mastered by these methods in less than a week. The same applies for any language. Almost anyone can master $80^0/0$ of everyday speech and text in any foreign language inside a week using the *Rhyming Slang Vocabulary* and the rest of the *Five x Five System*.

Remember to use all the sub-principles:

■   Make your images positive

- Use both sides of the brain
- Use all the senses
- Make the images interesting
- Give the associations rhyme and rhythm

All you have to do is take the foreign counterpart of each of the English words and ask yourself what English word sounds most like the foreign word. Visualise the image, together with the relevant *Rhyming Slang* image, and associate them in some meaningful way. Link each mother tongue — foreign language association together, using one of the chaining methods described in Chapter 3 and, within a very short time, you will have the mastery of all 200 words in your mind, ready to retrieve as and when you require. The very same *Rhyming Slang* words can then be used to learn an entirely different language, and then another, and so on. You could master every major language inside a year. Why hasn't this been done before? Because nobody has, hitherto, discovered a way to bridge the gap between the use of image association *and* the need to master the common function words.

I'm going to give you an example with the German language. The pages that follow contain the first fifty of the common words, together with their German translation and the relevant *Rhyming Slang* in each case. An example of the kinds of images you might use to relate these three elements of each association is also given. Study and rehearse them for five minutes and then test yourself. You'll be surprised how easy it is.

English Word	Rhyming slang	German translation	Image to visualise
a	straw & hay	*ein/eine,* pronounced ine	It sounds a bit like iron. imagine someone ironing straw and hay in a horsebox.
i	pastry & pie	ich, pronounced ik	Imagine someone saying a pie had made them sick, but don't pronounce the s. Alternatively, you might imagine them having pastry down their neck and it is making them itch, but they pronounce it ik.

it	drill & bit	es	Visualise someone drilling a hole in a metal letter S, perhaps to screw it on to a wall.
the	carrot & pea	*der, pronounced dare*	Imagine someone daring their friend to throw a carrot and pea at someone.
his	bubbles & fizz	seine, pronounced zine)	Visualise a sign depicting a glass of bubbling champagne.
on	Cambridge don	*auf, pronounced the way a Londoner would pronounce, Alf, i.e. with the I sounding like a w*	Visualise Alf Garnet as a Cambridge don.
so		(same as in English)	
as	trumpet & jazz	aus, pronounced as in mouse	Visualise the sign outside a Jazz house and hear the music in your head.
but	watchman and hut	aber	Imagine a member of the ABBA band in a watchman's uniform sitting in a watchman's hut.
him	barber and trim	Ihn, pronounced een	Imagine Ian Beale (East Enders Character) sitting in a barber's chair having a trim.
and	singer and band	und	Imaging a band playing under a bridge.
he	elbow and knee	er, pronounced air	Imaging someone with a transparent balloon in place of one of their elbow joints and one of their knee joints. It is, of course filled with air.
in		Same as in English	
was	why and because	warden, pronounced vairden	Imagine someone asking why this lion's den has a roundabout in it and receiving the reply

			because "It's a fair den"
be	leaf and tree	bin	Visualize a bin containing a leaf and a small tree.
one	current and bun	ein, pronounced as in nine	Imagine an iron currant falling on a bun with a figure 9 on it.
they	anchor and bay	sie, pronounced zee	Visualise a ship anchored out at sea.
you (sing)	cow and moo	du, pronounced doo	Imagine a cow with a cold and blocked nose trying to say moo, but it comes out as doo.
at	ball & bat	an	Imagine someone you know called Anne, playing with a bat and ball.
not	ink & blot	nicht, pronounced more or less as nicked except that the k is not show sharp or final.	Imagine a burglar being nicked because he left his fingerprint in a blot of ink from a bottle he had knocked over.
said	sleeper & bed	sagen, pronounced zergon	Visualize a gun (zer gun) with a nightcap on in bed
we	lock & key	wir, pronounced veer	Imaging a person who has had too much to drink trying to put their key into the lock on their front door. Intoxicated they veer to one side every time
call	brickie and wall	nemen, pronounced nearmun	Imagine a bricklayer with a welsh accent on a narrow scaffolding plank saying to his labourer "I'm too near mun"
has	curry madras	Er hat	Imagine a woman has remarked that if her husband ever cooked a meal for her she would eat her hat. He does so and winks at his friend who asks what is in the e curry he is serving. He whispers "'er hat"
if	bendy & stiff	wenn, pronounced	Imagine a mathematician drawing a venn diagram with

		ven	circular shapes made of wire. Some are bendy and some are stiff, as he demonstrates.
my	pan & fry	meine, pronounced miner	Imagine a miner frying breakfast underground
now	curtsy and bow	Jetzt, pronounced yetzt	Imagine the *yeti* curtsying then bowing
only	single & lonely	nur	Imagine asking someone if they are single and lonely and they reply *Nurr*
right	boxer & fight	recht, pronounced rekt	Imagine a German boxer slumping against the ropes and saying "I'm wrecked"
then	egg & hen	damals, pronounced darmals	Imagine a farmer looking at a squashed egg and chicken, which have been trampled by mules. He exclaims, "darm mules"
too	nail & screw	zwei, pronounced zvi	Imagine a carpenter fixing a nail and screw where indicated by a V marked on a piece of wood
well	clanger & bell	gut, pronounced goot	Imagine a Scotsman in a kilt (for the accent) in Germany. His wife asks "What is that ringing sound?" He points to a goat with a bell around its neck.
what	sailor & yacht	was, pronounced vas	Imaging the politician, Keith Vas on a yacht
your	lion & roar	dein, pronounced dine	Imagine a lion roaring for his dinner. Visualize it sitting there with knife and fork in hands.
back	partridge & sack	rucken	Imagine a partridge in a rucksack
big	shovel & dig	grobe, pronounced gross	Imagine someone digging with a shovel and finding 144 gold coins
can		cann, pronounced like English	

down	circus & clown	*can* daunen, pronounced dornen	Imagine a clown waking up when it is just getting light
her	cat & purr	sei, pronounced see	Visualise a cat floating happily in the sea, purring
little	ball & skittle	klein, pronounced kline	Visualise a really shiny, clean ball and a single skittle, perhaps someone cleaning it with a cloth comments, "No, it's not clean it's Kline.
make	baker & cake	marchen, pronounced marken	Visualize a baker marking a cake he has made
much	rabbit & hutch	viel, pronounced feel	Imagine feeling a rabbit in a hutch
no	shoelace & bow	nein, pronounced like the English word *nine*	Imagine someone teaching you to tie a bow. "You have to make a figure 9 with one piece of lace", they say.
see	biscuits & tea	sehen, pronounced zehen	Visualize a café counter assistant trying to hear what a quiet voiced customer is saying when he or she is asking for biscuits and tea.
their	barber & hair	ihr, pronounced eer	Imagine a barber clipping hair around someone's ears
there		dar	This pronunciation is quite similar to the English word, except that it starts with a *d* rather than a *t* and the vowel sound is *ar* not *ere*
up	saucer & cup	auf, pronounced as a cockney would pronounce Alf, making the l sound like a w	Visualise the character, Alf Garnet or the football manager Alf Ramsey balancing a saucer and cup on his head.

first	tyre & burst	erst, pronounced airst	Imagine the air actually making a sound like airst as it bursts. This might be the sound of a puncture which develops in a sudden burst.
go	lamp & glow	gehen, pronounced gayun	Imagine a weighing scale with a lamp that glows if there has been a weight gain since the last weighing. The lamp has the word GAIN printed on the shade
here		hier (same pronunciation as the English word)	
look	reader & book	gucken, pronounced gooken)	Sounds a bit like cooking. Visualise someone reading a Delia Smith cookbook.
more	music & score	mehr, pronounced mare	Visualise a horse reading a music score
must	iron & rust	mussen, pronounced moosen	Imagine a moose cast in iron and going rusty.
old	potter & mould	alt, pronounced as in altitude	Imagine a sentry guard shouting "Alt!" to a potter carrying a mould.
them	diamond & gem	sie, pronounced zee	Visualise a large diamond and another gemstone floating in the sea.
this	hit and miss	diese, Pronounced deeza	Imagine someone at a rifle range asking which are the targets they missed, and the range master answers " Dese are."
who	tiger & zoo	wer, pronounced vair	Imagine a tiger and mini zoo in a fairground.

Now I know this may sound complicated, but these are not easy words to form associations for, so persevere and it will pay dividends. The other words in the language will be easier to form straightforward associations for.

8

Memorising the Rules of Punctuation

CHAPTER 8

Punctuation causes many people problems - even adults. There are so many rules to contend with. This is how the *Five x Five System* can help you learn them quickly and easily, and store them in a form you'll never forget.

There are 27 basic rules of punctuation in the English language and, as you know, the short-term memory can only handle between five and nine bits of data at a time. The *Five x Five System* recommends that you, ideally, seek to store just five bits at once. Therefore, you need to chunk the spelling rules down so that you end up with a manageable number of categories. I have chunked the 27 rules below in terms of, firstly, the 11 punctuation marks in common use. Several have more than one use, making up the 27 common rules. A second layer of chunking has been carried out on the five categories - the *Five x Five System* recommended number.

Name of mark		Function	Final chunking criteria	
Colon	:	To introduce something. There are 3 instances: • examples • lists • elaborations		Category 1. Both terms include the word *colon*
Semicolon	;	The appearance of this punctuation mark suggests its function – halfway between a full stop and a comma. It is used where two grammatically distinct , but semantically interdependent sentences are merged into one.		
Hyphen	–	The hyphen has two uses: • to separate the parts of compound words • to split words so that the parts can be written on separate lines, thus, saving space.		Category 2. Both marks look the same
Dash	—	The dash has two uses. It signifies: • an abrupt break in speech • faltering speech		
Question mark	?	The question mark is used to signify a question		Category 3. Both include word *mark*
Exclamation mark	!	The exclamation mark is used to signify an exclamatory tone		
Apostrophe	'	The apostrophe has 3 uses - to indicate: • possession • omission of letters • plurals of numbers		Category 4. Both marks involve inverted comma
Speech marks	"	For enclosing direct speech		

Comma	**,**	There are 9 uses of the comma. Remember this by the fact that it looks like a figure 9. They can be sub-categorisesd into three kinds of function:

- enclosing things
- separating things
- indicating natural pauses

Commas are use to enclose:

- appositions
- personal names in speech
- words like: however, then and thus.

Commas are used to separate:

- clauses in a sentence
- items in a list
- direct speech and authorial voice
- the form of address and the body of a letter
- the body of a letter and the signature

Full stop   **.**   The full stop has 3 functions. It marks:

- the end of a sentence
- the end of a title, e.g. Mr. or Ms.
- an abbreviationi.

Brackets   **( )**   Brackets are used to enclose something which will aid comprehension of, but which is inconsistent with, the grammatical structure of a sentence.

9
Geography and the World Map

The more accurately you can get the world map into your head, the easier your geography studies will be. All the principles of the *Five x Five System* will help. Countries can be chunked into continents, island groups, unions of countries (UK, Soviet Union etc.), federations and trading partnerships (OPEC, G5, EU etc.).

Shapes can be used to denote the number of countries in each group, and acronyms and acrostics can help you recall their names.

The land masses of countries lend themselves well to image formation. Take Italy, for example. It looks like a boot. Russia looks like a bear. England looks like an old lady, Ireland looks like a lamb and Vietnam looks like a beckoning finger.

Add all the sense aspects to your images. Imagine the Premier of Russia roaring like a bear. Imagine eating spaghetti bolognaise from a boot. Have fun! The exercises lay down more and more roots in all the sense areas of the brain and the more roots, the more chance that your focal attention will find a pathway to what it is you want to recall.

Link all your images together into a story, poem or another chaining method. Use all the sub-principles of consolidation and if you are doing a geography exam then superimpose, in your mind's eye, the shapes and spatial arrangements on parts of the exam room to aid your recall.

10
Cueing Actors' Lines

The principles of the *Five x Five System* can be used to help actors remember their lines. Here's an example of how it is done, using what I call the OWETOA passage from Shakespeare's *Henry VI:*

> *0! Pity, God, this miserable age.*
> *What strategems, how fell, how butcherly;*
> *Erroneous, mutinous, and unnatural, This*
> *deadly quarrel daily doth beget! 0 boy! thy*
> *father gave thee life too soon, And hath bereft*
> *thee of thy life too late.*

This can be recalled very easily if you simply remember the word OWETOA. It's not a real word, but it has a sound that will stick in the mind, just as the similarly meaningless but widely used term SOH CAH TOA does to help pupils remember their trigonometry. Here's another example, using what I call the SABBAM STIR passage in *Henry IV.*

> *So, when the loose behaviour I throw off,*
> *And pay the debt I never promised, By how*
> *much better than my word I am. By so much*
> *shall I falsify men's hopes; And like bright*
> *metal on a sullen ground, My reformation;*
> *glittering o'er my fault,*
> *Shall show more goodly and attract more eyes*
> *Than that which hath no foil to set it off. I'll so*
> *offend to make offence a skill, Redeeming time*
> *when men think least I will.*

Actors can cue recall of this passage by associating it with the easily remembered term SABBAM STIR, each letter of which is also the first letter of its corresponding line.

There will be many cases where it is not possible to make an acronym with the initial letters of lines. You will recall that sub-principle 1:5 of the *Five x Five System* provides for such cases by using acrostics instead. As an example, take the following passage from *King Lear:*

> *Poor naked wretches, whereso'er you are,*
> *That bide the pelting of this pitiless storm,*
> *How shall your houseless heads and unfed sides,*
> *Your loop'd and window'd raggedness, defend you*
> *From seasons such as these? O! I have ta'en*
> *Too little care of this. Take physics, pomp;*
> *Expose thyself to feel what wretches feel,*
> *That thou mayst shake the superflux to them,*
> *And show the heavens more just.*

Recall of this can be cued easily by associating it with the sentence: *Polly took her yellow frog through every tiny alley.* The initial letter of each word corresponds to the initial letter of each line.

11

The Marshall System for Remembering Spellings

Some general rules for spelling are observable in the English language and learning them will help you recall the correct ways to spell certain words. The order in which 'i' and 'e' are generally juxtaposed has, for long, been enshrined in rhyme to make it memorable:

I before E, except
after C.

There are many others which are outside the scope of this book. (They can easily be learned from any book on English language). This book is concerned with spellings for which there are no observable rules and where particular spellings are exceptions to a rule. In the latter cases the rules can be more of a hindrance than a help. Memorising spellings usually involves learning a series of letters which, individually, mean little to the intellect. It is not surprising, therefore, that some people find the task hard. Often there are more than seven letters, so it exceeds the capacity of the average person's short-term memory and it won't get into long-term memory until some meaning is made of it.

The way to overcome these limitations is to find a way of chunking letters other than in the single word they spell. No point in using that to chunk the letters if you don't know how to spell it. The best way is to make an acrostic with the letters (sub-principle 1:5). Here is an example. Some people find difficulty with the word *because*. However, if you make this sentence with the letters, you will never forget the spelling again:

Big Elephants Can Always Upset Small Elephants.

Here you've taken a learning task that stretches the average person to the limit of their short-term memory capacity and chunked it so that it only takes up one-seventh of that capacity. Get the picture?

The pages that follow list the 200 most commonly misspelt words in the English language. Most of them can best be remembered by using an acrostic.

The Marshall Acrostic System for Commonly Misspelt Words

Spelling errors are sometimes due to there simply being too many letters for the short-term memory to handle, so the correct spelling never actually gets into long-term memory. When this is the case, making an acrostic out of the letters chunks many letters into a single unit of data. Short-term memory can then easily handle it and it will then reach long-term memory.

Absence	A big seat empty; no candidate entered.
Accidentally	A collision crash in driver's ear nearly took all logs last year.
Achieved	A cat hid in Eddie's van every day.
Aerial	All emails ring in a line.
Aggravate	A great gale rolled a van at the enemy.
Aggregate	All groups grouped round every group and totally engulfed.
Arctic	A really cold time in Canada.
Apparent	A polo pony at recent event near Toulouse.
Athletic	A tall healthy lass easily takes in challenge.
Awful	A war fought until lost.
Breathe	Breathes really easily and then he exhales.
Business	Building up sales is not easy say salesmen.
Choice	Claims her option is clearly easy.
Clothes	Clad like other ten holidaymakers each summer.
College	Class of lofty learners each getting examined.
Criticism	Claiming report is trash is claiming it seems mediocre.
Eighth	Even I got half the h's.
Eliminated	Every lamp is most illuminated near a tavern's entrance door.
Emphasize	Every man puts his action strategy in zone E.
Genius	Great engineers never improve under stress.
Guard	Go up and right down.
Heroes	Hinder every rider over every state.
Lose	Leave on some excursion.
Marriage	Mary and Robert reside in a great estate.
Mischievous	Most impish scamps can't help it every very old uncle says.
Murmur	Minute under-resonance, minute under-resonance.

Quiet	Quite unique in every town.
Really	Rusty engines always look like yellow.
Rhythm	Rap has yap time harmony mode.
Wednesday	When every dentist needs endless supplies-day.

Errors of recall rather than of storage

Some common misspellings are errors of recall rather than errors of storage. The problem is interference from similar storage. Errors in spelling the words *deceive, height* and *seize,* for example, are due to the common rule 'i' before 'e' except after 'c' getting in the way. These are actual exceptions to the rule and need to be learned as such. The associations you use should, ideally, refer to the fact that the spelling is an exception to the rule. For example, remembering the following sentence could help you with the word *seize:*

Seize the rule and prevent it applying.

Similarly, this sentence could help you remember the correct spelling of the word *deceive.*

Deceiving is a deceiving word, for it does not conform to the 'i' before 'e' rule.

Some words just don't sound anything like what the letters suggest. *Noticeable* is an example. People tend to miss out the 'e' in the middle. Where this is the case, make a habit of pronouncing the word literally, as you write it. Say Pee-op-lee, for example, as you write the word *people.* Then you deliberately store an association between writing the word and its literal pronunciation, albeit an inappropriate pronunciation. Here are some more:

amateur	am-a-tee-ur	synonymous	sy-nony-mous
colleagues	coll-ee-ay-gu-es	parliament	par-lia-ment
conscientious	con-cient-i-o-u-s	miniature	mini-a-ture
conscious	consc-i-o-u-s	familiar	fam-i- liar
restaurant	rest-ay-u-rant		

Some other tricks

Anxious	Few people have any difficulty with the first two letters. The rest can be remembered by this little trick:

I am anxious, because₊

    → X   I O U some money and you look ⌐

The cross represents both the word cross and the letter X.

Necessary	Remember one collar and two sleeves.
Woollen	Failure to use a double I is common. Remembering this little saying will help. I call my jumper Len Wool-Len.
Rhythm	Remember there are no vowels in this word.
Tendency	Develop a tenden - C To use a 'c' (rather than an 's').
Opinion	Think *onion pi* and then rearrange the letters like this

Knowledge	I know (a) ledge
Originally	Say to yourself, "The road was originally called Gin Ally".
Personnel	The personnel officer is called Nel. They call her Person-Nel.
Noticeable	All the letters of notice (and) able
Secretaries	Imagine your secretary kept their birth sign secret - secret Aries.

Wherever there is a palindrome, register it in your memory

A palindrome is a symmetrical group of letters. You will recall, from the treatment of principle 1.3, in chapter 1, that symmetrical things are remembered best.

Acc(ommo)dation   Sep(ara)te

(Ama)teur	Sev(ere)ly	(Two palindromes here, but this is the useful one)
(Ana)lysis	Sh(i(ni)n)g	(Two Palindromes)
An(nun)ciation	S(imi)lar	
(Appa)rent	Sinc(ere)ly	
(Arra)ngements	H(ono)(rar)y	(Two palindromes)
Beg(inni)ng	Hum(oro)us	
Coll(ege)	(immi)grate	
Comp(ara)tive	Ire(sis)tible	
Comp(ete)nt	Mainte(nan)ce	
Con(sis)tent	N(ece)ssary	
Cr(it(i)ci)sm (Two palindromes)	Op(ini)on	
D(ece)it	Or(igi)nally	
Def(ini)te	P(ara)llel	
Dec(isi)on	Perm(issi)ble	
El(imi)nated	Pers(eve)rence	
Exc(elle)nt	Po(ssess)es	(There are other palindromes here but this is the most useful one)

(Exe)rcise		Pr(ece)ding	
Expen(ses)		Pr(ef(e)re)nce	(Two palindromes)
Extr(eme)ly		Prel(imi)nary	
Feas(ib(i)li)ty	(Two Palindromes)	Surpr(isi)ng	
G(rammar)	(Almost the entire word is a palindrome)	S(ynony)mous	(Remember this word as having a 5 letter palindrome)
Pr(ivi)lege		Transf(erre)d	
Psych(olo)gy		Unn(ece)ssary	(Notice there is a double letter each side of the palindrome)
R(ef(e)rre)d	(Two Palindrome)		

Words with 'ici' palindromes
Med(ici)ne
Eff(ici)ently

Words with 'issi' palindromes
Perm(issi)ble
Om(issi)on

Words with 'ili' palindromes
Feasib(ili)ty
Fam(ili)ar

Spelling errors where only part of the word causes difficulty

Most spelling problems involve only part of the word. *Disappear,* for example, is a commonly misspelt word, but it is hard to imagine any non-dyslexic person failing to recall the correct spelling of the first three letters. In cases like this you only need to construct a mnemonic for the part that causes the problem. Here are some examples:

Acknowledge   Answer confirming knowledge (it's only the ac that people will get wrong, as long as they can spell the word knowledge).

Competent   It is the last syllable that people get wrong, so think - competent to put up a tent.

Bachelor   The error people make with this word is putting a t in it, so remember it by the phrase: Bachelors don't have tea.

Parallel   Remember the two parallel l's.

People sometimes have difficulty where there are pairs of double letters in a word. *Accommodation* is an example of this type of word.

People jump to the conclusion that only one of the letters is doubled. A simple rhyme overcomes this:

Accommodation and address
Have a double c, d, m and s.

Here are two more examples:

Committee   *Com-mit-tee*
            has doubles three
            m, t and double e

Possess   Possess *possesses*
          two double s' s.

12

Swatting for Exams

If you are swatting for exams you can make things a whole lot easier for yourself and still achieve 100% recall into the bargain if you use the principles of the *Five x Five System*. In the period leading up to examinations students tend to start cramming. This is normally the most inefficient, learning phase of the entire year. Why? Well, as you now know, the short-term memory has very limited capacity. Try to pack more in than it can handle and you will simply displace what is already there - the 'in one ear and out the other principle:

If you apply the chunking principles effectively, though, you will be able to overcome this problem and pack in as much as you want. You must avoid rushing to pack the material in until you've chunked it efficiently, on paper, first.

Secondly, use the hierarchy principle to chunk your chunks into larger chunks and then those into even larger ones. You can store massive amounts of information this way.

Using the *successive note reduction technique* serves the same purpose. Reduce sections of notes into single pages, then single pages into page sections, then page sections into paragraphs, then paragraphs into sentences, then sentences into phrases and then, finally, each phrase into the most appropriate key word. The test of the most appropriate key word is its power to cue your recall of the rest of the phrase.

Use shapes, acronyms and acrostics and you'll be able to recall every single detail.

You've got to, therefore, get the information into long-term memory and in a form that will stick there. *Image association* is the key and you should use all the sub-principles to make your images mnemonically effective.

Use one of the chaining methods to link all the images together and follow the principles of effective memory consolidation. Don't start at the beginning of lists, or you'll never learn the ends. Start in the middle, then go to the end, and then do the beginning. Reinforce your storage, or you will be wasting your time and effort. If your exam is in the morning, swat right up until the night before and then switch off until the exam starts the next day.

Mentally place cues all over the exam room or in another room that you can visualise in the exam room.

Utilise all the recall tricks, as necessary - tip of the tongue, backtracking, relaxation - and don't hesitate to reconstruct if need be.

After the exam, forget all about it. Post-mortemising will only lead to storage of negative emotions. This will damage confidence for future exams and confidence is a significant factor in memory recall.

13

Remembering Long Numbers

If you should wish to remember long numbers (there are world records that people strive to break), here's how to do it.

Chunk the number into fives and then break each of these into a group of two and a group of three digits. Use the number/letter matching system to form an image of a person (famous or someone you know) to represent the first pair of digits and use the *Image Vocabulary for Numbers* to form an image for the triad of digits. You can then form a subject and predicate statement for each group of five digits in the long number. Use the Greek method of loci to store each of the subject-predicate images in a selected location. Use a well-practised journey around a site of appropriate size. This might be anything from a house, at the one extreme, to a city, at the other. You can then remake your journey, seeing and translating each of the images as you go.

14

Remembering Formulae

Mathematical formulae often have symmetry, or at least some easily recognisable shape. Take the formula for coefficient of determination, for example,

$$r^2 \quad \frac{\Sigma(\hat{Y} - \bar{Y})^2}{\Sigma(Y - \bar{Y})^2}$$

This has some degree of symmetry, doesn't it? The one accent missing from the bottom term is likely to do more to help than hinder your memory, for you will have noticed it is an exception to the symmetry.

Here's another example of how you can use memory tricks to help you with your math. The way to multiply a pair of binomial expressions is to draw a smiling face around them. Watch.

$$(x + 5)\ (x + 4)$$

Multiply the pairs connected by lines and simplify: $x^2 + 9x + 20$

Other formulae lend themselves to acronym or acrostic treatment. For example, a way to remember the three main trigonometrical ratios is SOH, CAH, TOA.

$$S = \frac{O}{H} \quad C = \frac{A}{H} \quad T = \frac{O}{A}$$

Alternatively, you can memorise it as: **S**ome **O**f **H**arry's **C**ars **A**re **H**aving **T**rouble **O**n **A**cceleration.

Memory tricks can help people at any age. If you are a child learning your multiplication tables, or an adult who has never learnt them, here's an easy way to get the *nine times table* into your head. Notice that the digits of every product in the table add up to nine:

$2 \times 9 = 18 (1 + 8 = 9)$
$3 \times 9 = 27 \ (2+7=9)$
$4 \times 9 = 36 (3 + 6 = 9)$

What is more, up to 9×9 all the first digits in the products are consecutive and run one behind the multiplier — 1, 2, 3, etc. All you have to do to get them right is deduct one from the multiplier and add whatever digit is needed to make them add up to 9.

15

Remembering Playing Cards

If you want to be able to recall card sequences in whole shuffled packs, here's how to do it. You need to use all the principles of the *Five x Five System,* but well start with image formation this time.

Image formation
On pages 110-14 you will find a list of all the cards in a pack, together with three images for each. The first is a *subject* image, the second a *verb* image and the third an *object* image - all the elements of a sentence in each case.

Each image is based on a two-letter card identifier. The first letter is based on the card number, using the number-letter matching system, i.e. substituting the number with the corresponding letter of the alphabet (see page 32). The second letter is the initial letter of the suit. For example, the three of clubs becomes C C and the four of hearts becomes D H. The letters A, K, L and M are used for the Aces, Jacks, Queens and Kings.

Consequently, in the list you will find the Ace of Spades (AS) as Abe Simpson and the two of Diamonds is Big Daddy, etc. Anyway, all you have to do is learn the list. For example, the three images for the Ace of Spades are *Abe Simpson, acting suspiciously* and *alphabet soup.* The three images for the seven of Hearts are *Gloria Hunniford, goose-stepping haughtily and glass hammer.* The three images for the four of Diamonds are *Doris Day, dancing drunkenly* and *dotty Dalmatian.*

Chunking
What you will also need is a loci system. You need to plan a short journey in your mind with 18 locations in it. It might be a regular shopping trip, taking in the bank, the paper shop, the bookie's and so on. It might be a regular delivery round, or it might be a pub crawl. All that is necessary is that the journey has 18 stops in it.

As you see the cards being dealt out, whether it is you or someone else who is dealing them, chunk them into groups of three by forming a sentence for each triad. Use the appropriate subject image for the first card, the relevant verb image for the second and the appropriate object image for the third. Then you go back to subject images to begin to form the second sentence.

As you make each sentence, visualise the scene you have so described and store it in the next consecutive location in your loci system. For example:

Captain Hook bathing splashingly with a *double scotch,* at the Flying Horse;

Isla St Clare hosing drenchingly a flying duck at the Plough; *Doris Day climbing downwardly* on to a *door handle* at the Farmers' Arms; and so on.

When the whole pack has been dealt, re-walk the journey and see in your mind's eye the scene stored at each place. As you do so, decode the one-sentence descriptor into the relevant three card sequence in each case.

If you fail to recall any of them, have them put to one side and, at the end, run over the cards that you have recalled. The cards not yet accounted for will almost certainly jog your memory sufficiently to recall the sequences you missed out. The Marshall system is easy; you'll surprise yourself.

Vocabulary of Images for Playing Cards

Ace	Spades	Abe Simpson	Acting suspiciously	Alphabet soup
2	Spades	Barry Sheen	bathing splashingly	black sheep
3	Spades	Carol Smiley	Creeping slowly	Creepy spider
4	Spades	Donald Sinden	Dancing sexily	Double scotch
5	Spades	Eric Sykes	Elbowing sneakily	Eastern sun
6	Spades	Frank Skinner	Flying supersonically	Fresh salad

7	Spades	Gary Sobers	Growing slowly	Giant squid
8	Spades	Homer Simpson	Hiking smartly	HP sauce
9	Spades	Isla St Clare	Inhaling sharply	Indian scalp
10	Spades	Jerry Springer	Juggling swiftly	Jazzy saxaphone
Jack	Spades	Katy Scarlet	Kissing sweetly	Killer shark
Queen	Spades	Lily Savage	Leaping sportily	Large sack
King	Spades	Marge Simpson	Massaging soothingly	Mine shaft
Ace	Hearts	Alex Higgins	Asking humbly	Alpine horn
2	Hearts	Bob Hope	Bugling happily	Black hat
3	Hearts	Captain Hook	Chomping hungrily	Clothes horse
4	Hearts	Dirty Harry	Dropping heavily	Door handle
5	Hearts	Englebert Humperdink	Exercising heartily	Elephants hoof
6	Hearts	Frankie Howard	Fasting honourably	Feathery hawk
7	Hearts	Gloria Hunniford	Goose-stepping haughtily	Glass hammer
8	Hearts	Hulk Hogan	Hoisting highly	High hat

9	Hearts	Irene Handle	Interrupting hastily	Ice hotel
10	Hearts	Jimmy Hill	Joking humorously	Jew's harp
Jack	Hearts	Kirk Hammet	Knitting helpfully	Kinky harness
Queen	Hearts	Liz Hurley	Laughing heartily	Long hair
King	Hearts	Mata Hari	Morphing hauntingly	Muddy hippo
Ace	Diamonds	Arthur Daly	Absconding deviously	Angry dog
2	Diamonds	Big Daddy	Bashing dominantly	Baby's diaper
3	Diamonds	Celine Dion	Climbing downwardly	cabbage - patch doll
4	Diamonds	Doris Day	Dancing drunkenly	Dotty Dalmatian
5	Diamonds	Eliza Doolittle	Exploring daringly	Editor's desk
6	Diamonds	Freddy Davies	Flirting devilishly	Flying duck
7	Diamonds	George Dawes	Guarding dutifully	Green door
8	Diamonds	Humpty dumpty	Hosing drenchingly	Hunter's dart
9	Diamonds	Ian Drury	Icing decoratively	Indigo daffodil
10	Diamonds	Johnny Dankworth	Juggling dextrously	Jurassic dinosaur

Jack	Diamonds	Kirk Douglas	Keying desperately	Kicking a drum
Queen	Diamonds	Les Dawson	Lazing dreamily	Living dodo
King	Diamonds	Matt Dillon	Marching doggedly	Millennium dome
Ace	Clubs	Alice Cooper	Appealing charitably	Army cadet
2	Clubs	Bill Clinton	Balancing cleverly	Birthday cake
3	Clubs	Charlie Chaplin	Can-canning confidently	Chirping canary
4	Clubs	Dot Cotton	Driving courteously	Desert camel
5	Clubs	Eric Clapton	Entertaining cleverly	Electric chair
6	Clubs	Frank Carson	Falling clumsily	False cleavage
7	Clubs	Geoff Capes	Grunting crudely	Grandfather clock
8	Clubs	Hilary Clinton	Halving carefully	Hot curry
9	Clubs	Ian Carmichael	Ironing creasingly	Ice-cream cornet
10	Clubs	James Cagney	Jousting carefully	Jammed cannon
Jack	Clubs	Keith Chegwin	Kicking childishly	Kitchen cupboard
Queen	Clubs	Lesley Crowther	Looking cutely	Lumpy custard

| King | Clubs | Michael Caine | Miming capriciously | Mouldy cheese |

16

Remembering Jokes

You often hear people say, 'I can never remember jokes.' Most people would like to be able to remember them, because always having a joke to tell makes a person popular.

How can the *Five x Five System* help? Well, there are two kinds of 'not being able to remember jokes':

■ not being able to call them to mind
■ not being able to remember how to tell them when you do.

Failure to call jokes to mind

If it's the first one that causes you the most difficulty, then it's a case of retrieval failure. You will recall that there is a whole bag of tricks for this in the *Five x Five System*. The most relevant sub-principle is 5:3 — *looking for cues*. You will recall that you can deliberately set up cues, so that they are available as and when you need them. When you hear a joke you would like to retell, visualise the setting in which you would like to retell it. Then hang a reminder on some part of the image. Suppose it is at your local pub that you would like to retell a joke about a cowboy. Mentally see the cowboy hanging his hat over one of the wall lamps, or some other odd place. If you would like to tell the boozy giraffe joke at the office, imagine a giraffe's neck appearing outside the window. This will spontaneously jog your memory when you are actually at the office and looking towards the window. If others at the office are telling jokes, look around the room and items of furniture and other features will spark off recall of however many jokes you have, over time, stored in this way.

Failure to recall how a joke goes

If this is your problem, then what you need to store is
(a) the punch line
(b) how to get there
(c) the first sentence verbatim

95

The last of these will act as a cue for the rest of the joke.

You need to find a way of hanging each one of these on to items of furniture or parts of the room in which you envisage telling the joke. Then, when you are in that situation, you can just look around the room to jog your memory.

17

Remembering Birthdays and Anniversaries

Many people have difficulty remembering birthdays and anniversaries. This is because it is a very different kind of memory problem from most others. It is not so much about retrieval quality; it is about the ability to self-alert, to start the retrieval process off. We don't have a reliable mental mechanism for making that happen.

The answer lies in sub-principle 5:3 of the *Five x Five System* — using cues. Here you have to build the cues into your recall context (where you will be expected to remember the occasion) and build them in so that they are so obvious that you cannot possibly miss them. That means they have to be, not mental cues, but actual physical ones. The best cues are aspects of your immediate environment that have been conspicuously and incongruently altered. Wrap a rubber band around your key ring, so that it prevents it fitting into the ignition and you'll ask yourself, 'Why did I do that?' Put a knot in your handkerchief. Put your watch on the wrong wrist, or your ring on the wrong finger. Place a note on your car seat (this is better than the dashboard, because you've got to remove it to sit down). Jam a piece of paper into the opening of your briefcase. Tie a knot in the strap of your handbag.

These kinds of tactics should be enough. The mind only needs a little jog. The connection doesn't have to be complete.

SOME COMMON FORENAMES AND THEIR MEANINGS

Alan	Rock. This name means the same as Peter, so to avoid confusion visualise the person as made of ash rock or rock formed from volcano lava. This is relatively light and less dense than most rock.
Alex	Defender and warrior. Visualise the person as a bodyguard.
Amanda	Loveable. Visualise the person being kissed by everyone.
Andrew	Warrior. Visualise the person as a warrior.
Angel	An angel. Visualise the person as an angel.
Anne	God has favoured me with a baby. Visualise woman holding a baby.
Anthony	Flower. Visualise the person as a flower.
Audrey	Noble and strong. Visualise the person dressed as a nobleman lifting heavy weights.
Barry	Short form of Finbar, meaning white head. Visualise the person with a white head.
Basil	Royal. Visualise the person wearing a crown.
Bernard	Visualise the person as a bear.
Bethany	House of figs. Visualise the person in a house of figs.
Bianca	White, pure. Visualise the person in a white gown.
Bob	Pet name for Robert, which means fame Visualise the person's image as a dog, or some other pet, in lights, above the door of a theatre.
Chantel	Boulder. Visualise the person made of a huge boulder.
Chris	Short form of Christopher. Visualise the person as a very short St Christopher.
Christopher	Christ to bear. Legend has it that St Christopher bore the Christ child over a stream and is regarded as patron saint of travellers. Visualise the person as St Christopher.
Claire	Derives from Clara, meaning famous. Visualise the

	person with their image in lights.
Claude	Lame. Visualise the person lame.
Cliff	A cliff. Visualise the person standing on a cliff.
Colin	Short form of Nicholas, which means victory and people. Visualise the person as very short and at the head of a victorious army.
Courtney	A short nose. Visualise the person with a short nose.
Dale	Dweller in a dale or valley. Visualise the person yodeling.
David	The name of the greatest of the Israelite kings (David and Goliath). Visualise the person killing Goliath with his sling.
Derek	A name introduced to Britain by Flemish cloth-makers. Visualise the person standing at a weaving loom.
Diane	Name of the Roman goddess of the moon. Visualise the person in a Temple of Diana.
Dick	Short for Richard. Introduced by the French because they had difficulty pronouncing the r in Richard. Visualise the person as a hard and powerful Frenchman.
Donald	World and rule. Visualise the person standing on top of the globe.
Douglas	Black stream. Visualise the person standing in a black stream.
Edward	Riches and guard. Visualise the person as a sentry guard with gold bracelets and rings.
Elaine	Welsh fawn. Visualise the person as a young deer.
Elizabeth	God is my oath Visualise the person swearing an oath on the Bible.
Elsie	Short form of Elizabeth. Visualise the person as a very short person swearing an oath.
Fiona	Wine. Visualise the person drinking wine.
Francis	Derives from Francesco, meaning a Frenchman. Visualise the person as a theatrical Frenchman, with onions around his neck.
Frank	Member of the Frank tribe (so called because of the shape of the spears they used). Visualise the person holding a spear.
Fraser	Earliest source known is the strawberry.

	Visualise the person with a strawberry for a head.
Gary	Spear. Visualise the person holding a spear, or with a head like the head of a spear.
Geoffrey	Territory stranger. Visualise the person as a stranger, at whom everyone is looking.
George	Farmer. Visualise the person in wellingtons and holding a sheherd's crook.
Geraldine	Feminine form of Gerald, meaning spear and rule. Visualise the woman holding a spear.
Graham	Homestead in a gravelly place. Visualise the person walking up a very gravelly drive to their home.
Harold	Army ruler. Visualise the person as a military dictator.
Harry	Pet name for Henry, which means home ruler. Visualise the person as a dog, or other pet, ruling over their home.
Harvey	Battleworthy. Visualise the person as a tank.
Hayley	Dweller in a hay clearing. Visualise the person living in a tent in the middle of a hay barn.
Heather	The shrub of this name. Visualise the person wearing a sprig of heather.
Helen	Sunbeam. Visualise the person in a ray of sunshine.
Henry	Home ruler. Visualise the person ruling over their home.
Herbert	Army, bright, famous. Visualise the person as a soldier whose image is in lights.
Hilary	Cheerful. Visualise the person laughing.
Irene	Peaceable. Visualise the person relaxing in peace.
Iris	Rainbow. Visualise the person through a rainbow.
Isobel	Spanish form of Elizabeth, which means God is my oath. Visualise the person as a Spaniard taking an oath on the Bible.
Jack	Pet form of John, which derives its meaning from John the Baptist. Visualise the person as a dog, or some other pet, baptizing someone.
Jane	Feminine form of John. Visualise the woman in the river baptizing someone.
Janet	Diminutive of Jane. Visualise the person as a very short woman in the river baptizing

someone.

Jennifer	Cornish form of Guinevere, King Arthur's unfaithful wife.
Jim	Short form of James which means heel grabber. Visualise the person as a very short person grabbing someone's heel.
Joan	Contracted form of Johanna. It was popularised by stories of Joan of Arc. Visualise the person as Joan of Arc.
John	God is gracious. Its popularity probably derives from John the Baptist. Visualise the person in a river baptizing people.
Keith	Wood. Visualise the person as made of wood.
Kenneth	Born of fire. Visualise the person being born out of fire.
Kimberly	Named after a South African town, which was the scene of battle in the Boer War. Visualise the person as a soldier in that battle.
Lee	Dweller in a clearing of a wood. Visualise the person in that setting.
Len	Short form of Leonard, meaning lion and strong, brave and hardy. Visualise the person as a very short lion.
Les	Short form of Leslie, which means dweller in a garden of hollies. Visualise the person as very short and in a garden of hollies.
Linda	Weak, tender and soft. Visualise the person as tender and soft.
Louis	Fame and warrior. Visualise the image of the person in an advert for a film about his life as a famous warrior.
Maggie	Pet name for Margaret. Visualise the person as a pet with a string of pearls around her neck.
Margaret	Pearl. Visualise the person with a string of pearls around her neck, or standing in an oyster shell.
Mary	Derives from Miriam, meaning drop of the sea or star of the sea. Visualise the person dropping into the sea, or as a star shining on the sea.
Matthew	Gift of God. Visualise the person being unwrapped in a gift parcel.
Melanie	Black or dark. Visualise the person as such.
Morris	Anglicised form of Moses, which is an Egyptian

	name meaning born of a certain god, like Rameses. Visualise the person as an Egyptian Pharaoh.
Neil	Cloud, passionate, or champion. Visualise the person riding on a cloud.
Nicholas	Victory and people. Visualise the person at the head of a victorious army.
Nicole	Feminine form of Nicholas. Visualise the woman at the head of a victorious army.
Noel	Birthday of the Lord. Visualise the person dressed up as Father Christmas.
Norman	North man or Norseman, i.e. Viking. Visualise the person as such.
Oliver	Olive tree. Visualise the person standing under an olive tree.
Peter	Rock. Visualise the person made out of rock - perhaps seaside rock.
Philip	Lover of horses. Visualise the person as such.
Rachel	A ewe. Visualise the person as such.
Richard	Power and hard. Visualise the person as such.
Robert	Fame and bright. Visualise the person's image in lights.
Stephen	Garland, crown. Visualise the person wearing a floral crown.
Stuart	Steward in a manor, or royal household. Visualise the person as a butler.
Susan	Anglicised form of Susanna, meaning lily, or rose. Visualise the person with rose or lily petals around her face.
Terry	Tribe and power. Visualise the person at the head of a tribe.
Thomas	Twin. Visualise the person in duplicate.
Valerie	Strong and healthy. Visualise the person as an athlete.
Victor	Conquerer. Visualise the person as the winner of a fight.
Wendy	Invented by the author of Peter Pan. Visualise the person as Peter Pan's Wendy.
Will	Pet name for William, meaning desire and helmet. Visualise the person as a dog, or some other pet, wearing a battle helmet.
William	Will, desire and helmet. Visualise the person wearing a battle helmet.

APPENDIX 2

SOME COMMON SURNAMES AND THEIR MEANINGS

Allen
Rock. Visualise the person made of rock. To avoid confusion with the name Peter, which also means rock, image this person made completely of rock while a person with the name Peter is made only partly of rock, perhaps from the neck up (A for Allen = A for all and P for Peter = P for part.).

Baker
Maker of bread. Visualise the person baking bread.

Baldwin
Bald person. Visualise the person as such.

Banks
From Gaelic *bruachan,* meaning corpulent. Visualise the person as fat around the middle.

Brown
Brown haired and swarthy complexion. Visualise the person as such.

Caldwell
Cold spring well. Visualise the person taking a dip in a cold spring well.

Campbell
Crooked mouth. Visualise the person with a crooked mouth.

Carpenter
Worker of wood. Visualise the person as such.

Clark
A minor cleric. Visualise the person as such.

Cooper
Descendant of someone who makes wooden tubs. Visualise the person helping their father build wooden tubs.

Davis
Beloved. Visualise the person with kiss marks all their cheek.

Edwards
Prosperity and guard. Visualise the person guarding riches.

Flynn
Red haired. Visualise the person as such.

Gardener
A gardener of food crops. Visualise the person as such.

Gordon
Border county Scot. Visualise the person as such.

Grant
A tall person. Visualise the person as such.

Green
Dweller by a village green or green man role in May Day celebrations.

Hall
Worker at a manor house. Visualise the person as a servant.

Harris
Inhabitant of Harrow, known for its pagan temple.

Harrison
Child of inhabitant of Harrow. Harrow is famous for its pagan temple, so visualise the

person as a child with a sun badge on its forehead, suggesting it is from a family of sun worshippers.

Hill	Dweller by, or on a hill. Visualise the person as such.
Hughes	Derived from *aodh,* meaning fire. Visualise the person made of fire.
James	In Genesis, this name is associated with the word heel. Visualise the person grabbing someone's heel.
Jones	Welshman. Visualise the person in Welsh national costume.
Keith	Wood. Visualise the person made of wood.
Kennedy	Descendant of someone armoured and helmeted. Visualise the person wearing a battle helmet.
Kerr	Left-handed. Visualise the person writing with their left hand.
Kidd	Goat herd. Visualise the person as such.
King	A king. Visualise the person wearing a crown.
Ladd	A young servant. Visualise the person as such.
Lake	Dweller by a lake. Visualise the person as such.
Lewis	Warrior (in Wales it is also associated with a lion). Visualise the person as a warrior wearing a lion's head.
Lock	(and similar names) Someone with curly hair. Visualise the person as such.
Lovejoy	A happy person. Visualise the person as such.
Mason	Stone mason. Visualise the person as such.
McLaughlin	(and similar names) Person who came from a Lakeland, i.e. Viking. Visualise the person as such.
Mitchell	(and similar names) One of a tribe of ingenious etymologists. Visualise the person demonstrating something about the structure of a word on a blackboard.
Mole	Like a mole, or short sighted, or someone who has a prominent mole. Visualise the person as such.
Moor	Moorland dweller. Visualise the person as such, perhaps gathering furze.
Morgan	Sea bright. Visualise the person with skin the colour of a bright sea.
Morris	Descendant of a man of Moorish race, dark and swarthy. Visualise the person as a child

	with these characteristics.
Murphy	Sea warrior. Visualise the person on the bridge of a warship.
Neil	(and similar names) Derived from Niall, meaning cloud or champion. Visualise the person riding on a cloud.
Knight	A knight in armour. Visualise the person as such.
Nightingale	Good singer. Visualise the person singing.
Niven	Saint. Visualise the person with a halo.
Oakley	Dweller in an oak clearing. Visualise the person as such.
Oliver	Olive tree. Visualise the person by an olive tree.
Page	Page-boy. Visualise the person as such.
Painter	Painter of walls and windows. Visualise the person as such.
Parker	Nosy person. Visualise the person as such.
Peck	Measurer of dry goods. Visualise the person measuring corn.
Perrett	Pear-shaped head. Visualise the person with a pear-shaped head.
Perry	Dweller by pear trees. Visualise the person in a house by some pear trees.
Phillips	Son of Philip, the horse lover.
Pigeon	Hunter of wood pigeon. Visualise the person as such.
Porter	Doorkeeper. Visualise the person as such.
Price	Person who fixes prices. Visualise the person as a bookmaker on a racecourse.
Quinn	Leader. Visualise the person leading an army.
Roberts	Famous or bright. Visualise the person's image in lights above the door of a theatre.
Randall	Raven Wolf. Visualise the person as an animal that is half wolf and half raven.
Riley	Sporting. Visualise the person in sporting clothing.
Roberts	Famous or bright. Visualise the person's image in lights, above the door of a theatre.
Robinson	Son of someone famous or bright. Visualise the person standing beside a famous or bright father or mother. If bright is your choice, you could visualise the parent wearing doctoral robes and hat, and the child wearing a child's version of the same.
Shaw	Wolf. Visualise the person as such.

Sullivan	Black-eyed. Visualise the person as such.
Taylor	A maker of clothes. Visualise the person sewing or measuring for a suit.
Thomas	Twin. Visualise the person in duplicate.
Thompson	Descendant of Thomas, which means twin.
Turner	Wood turner. Visualise the person working a lathe.
Walker	Walker on cloth to make it cleaner and thicker. Visualise the person doing so.
Ward	Watchman or guard. Visualise the person as such.
White	Visualise the person with white hair and complexion.
Williams	Descendant of William the Conqueror. Visualise the person as William the Conqueror.
Wilson	Protection. Visualise the person as a bodyguard.
Wood	Forester. Visualise the person chopping down a tree.

APPENDIX 3

100 IMAGES FOR NUMBERS

1	Lead
2	Nag
3	Mag
4	Rag
5	Sack
6	Bag
7	Tap
8	Fan
9	Page
10	Low. Visualise a limbo dancer limboing under the bar
11	Lilo. Common name for a blow-up sunbed
12	Lino
13	Lamp
14	Lard
15	Last. (Tool used by a cobbler to hold upturned shoes)
16	Lab. (Common name for laboratory)
17	Lettuce
18	Lift
19	Lip
20	Noah
21	Nail
22	Noon. (When the sun is overhead)
23	Name. (Perhaps visualize a name badge)
24	Nerd. (Visualise an anorak-wearing computer buff)
25	Nest
26	Nib
27	Net
28	Knife
29	Nip
30	Moo. (Imagine a cow mooing)

32	Man. (Perhaps visualise da Vinci's symbol)
33	Mime. (Visualise a mime performer)
34	Mire. (A swamp)
35	Mice.
36	Mobile. Mobile phone
37	Mat
38	Move. (Perhaps visualise a furniture removal van)
39	Muppet
40	Row. (Visualise people rowing a boat)
41	Rail
42	Rain
43	Ram
44	Rear. (Imagine a horse rearing)
45	Rust
46	Rib
47	Rat
48	Raft
49	Rip
50	Sow. (Visualise a farmer sowing seeds by hand)
51	Sail
52	Sign
53	Seam
54	Sore
55	Sauce. (Visualise a bottle of sauce)
56	Sub. (Submarine)
57	Sit
58	Safe
59	Sip. (Visualise a person sipping through a straw)
60	Bow
61	Bale
62	Bin
63	Beam
64	Bear

65	Bass. (The fish called bass)
66	Bib
67	Bat
68	Beef
69	Bap. (The Welsh name for a circular bread roll)
70	Toe
71	Tail
72	Tan
73	Tame. (Imagine successfully taming a lion)
74	Tear
75	Tease
76	Tub
77	Tattoo
78	Tiff
79	Tape
80	Foe
81	fool
82	phone
83	foam
84	fair
85	face
86	Fab. (Visualise FAB 1 - Lady Penelope's car)
87	Fat
88	Fife. (The musical instrument)
89	fop (An effeminate man of the regency period)
90	Pooh. (Visualise Pooh Bear)
91	Pail
92	Pin ((Visualise a safety pin)
93	Poem. (Visualise a poem written on a scroll, or someone reciting a poem)
94	Pair. Perhaps visualize a pair of shoes
95	Piece. (Perhaps visualize a piece of a jigsaw
96	Pub
97	Pot
98	Pave (Visualise a workman laying paving stones)

99   Peace pipe
100   Loom (Visualise a weaving loom)

Guinness Book of Records

Memorising the pi constant is an ongoing preoccupation for national and world record chasers. In 1979 the British Pi record was held by Michael Poultney, of Burnley, at about 3,500 digits, before being broken by Chreighton Carvello, a nurse from Middlesborough, who memorized it to 20,083 digits. This record held for approximately 20 years until it was broken by David Thomas, a fireman from Leeds, who set a new record of 22,500 digits. The writer was the principal invigilator in this and many other such events.

If you fancy having a go yourself, here are the first 1000 digits to get you started. Use the techniques described in the first five chapters of this book to build stories with images representing the numbers.

3.14159265358979323846264338327950288419716939937510
58209749445923078164062862089986280348253421170679
82148086513282306647093844609550582231725359408128
48111745028410270193852110555964462294895493038196
44288109756659334461284756482337867831652712019091
45648566923460348610454326648213393607260249141273
72458700660631558817488152092096282925409171536436
78925903600113305305488204665213841469519415116094
33057270365759591953092186117381932611793105118548
07446237996274956735188575272489122793818301194912
98336733624406566430860213949463952247371907021798
60943702770539217176293176752384674818467669405132
00056812714526356082778577134275778960917363717872
14684409012249534301465495853710507922796892589235
42019956112129021960864034418159813629774771309960
51870721134999999983729780499510597317328160963185 9
50244594553469083026425223082533446850352619311881
71010003137838752886587533208381420617177669147303
59825349042875546873115956286388235378759375195778
18577805321712268066130019278766111959092164201989

Michael Poultney set a British record for Pi
Memory recall at 7,769 digits in 1979
Drawing by Peter Marshall

Chreighton Carvello set a new British record for Pi Memory recalling 20,,083 digits, a record he held for approximately 20 years.
Drawing by Peter Marshall

The Great Memory Show

The Great Memory Show ran for several years in the late 1990s. It was created and hosted by Dr Peter Marshall, primarily as a means of gaining easy access to a population of people in whom superior memory quality might be found, for the purpose of on-going research at London University.

Memory performers were invited to perform on stage in front of National Television cameras and show the public their techniques. There was also a charitable component, in that a percentage of the revenue for the show was donated to the Alzheimer's Disease Society.

The research project had, for many years, sought such populations from groups such as Oxford and Cambridge history and law graduates, taxi drivers, Mensa members and so on, but finding people with naturally superior memory quality proved to be as difficult as finding needles in haystacks. Then Dr Marshall had the idea of instead of looking for them let them look for us and created the Great Memory Show for the purpose.

Natural memory quality (what the research project was looking for) and trained memory quality are two different things. The extent to which this population were technique users, as opposed to natural mnemonists would be evident in the show, because they would be actually demonstrating how they achieved their high levels of recall.

The show did provide useful data on natural memory quality, a good example of which is Creighton Carvello. Despite using techniques to achieve and hold the National Pi Record for 20 years, he also demonstrated superior iconic memory quality (something with which no techniques can assist) when he subsequently set a record for recalling a staggering 19 digits after a ½ second exposure.

HOW TO STUDY AND LEARN
Your practical guide to effective study skills
Dr Peter Marshall

Are you thinking of studying or training for an important qualification? Do you know the best techniques for studying and learning to ensure you achieve the best results as quickly as possible? Whether you are at college or university, doing projects or assignments, writing essays, receiving continuous assessment or preparing for exams this is the book for you. Now in its third edition, this practical book covers getting your thinking right, organising yourself properly, finding and processing the information you need, reading effectively, developing good writing skills, thinking creatively, motivating yourself, and more. Whatever your subject, age or background, start now and turn yourself into a winning candidate.

UNLOCKING YOUR POTENTIAL
How to master your mind, life and destiny
Dr Peter Marshall

If you really want to unlock your potential and become master of your own life, you will need to remove the barriers to success, including your own narrow expectations and those imposed by others. This book will introduce you to techniques for overcoming the limiting effects of past conditioning, misguided or obsolete teachings and repressed conflicts. You will learn how to develop your creativity, improve your ability to solve problems and manage your social contacts to facilitate success.

MAXIMISING YOUR MEMORY
How to train yourself to remember more
Dr Peter Marshall

A powerful memory brings obvious advantages in educational, career and social terms. At school and college, those certificates that provide a passport to a career depend heavily on what you can remember in the exam room. In the world of work, being able to recall details which slip the minds of colleagues will give you a competitive edge. In addition, one of the secrets of being popular with customers and friends is to remember their names and the little things that make them feel they matter to you. This popular book, now in its second edition, explains clearly how you can maximise your memory in order to achieve your academic, professional and personal goals.

UNDERSTANDING HUMAN MEMORY
What it is and how it Works
Dr Peter Marshall

This book explores the subject of human memory in all its dimensions – how it works physiologically and chemically, how it develops by conditioning and training, how it sometimes plays tricks on us to protect us, how it can fail through physiological damage and what we can do if it does. Now in its second edition, it will be essential reading for students of psychology, nursing, medicine and other disciplines concerned with understanding and management of human behaviour.

RESEARCH METHODS
How to choose and use the right methods
Dr Peter Marshall

All social science courses offered at universities or colleges include a research methods module, for which students are expected to purchase a research methods book. These are invariably weighty and expensive at a time when student funds are stretched. Dr Marshall has produced a reader-friendly, plain English and value-for-money solution. In this second edition, he explains the various methods available to social researchers and the basic principles, strengths and weakness involved in the use of both quantitative and qualitative methods. Whether you are new to the subject or an established practitioner this book should prove valuable. Dr Marshall has had many years' experience in research and teaching in universities and colleges

A HANDBOOK OF HYPNOTHERAPY
A practitioner's guide
Dr Peter Marshall

In simple, plain English style, this book will guide you through the entire subject – the theories underlying hypnosis, the disorders it can be used to treat, the wide range of procedures and the protocols for treating different conditions. You will find step-by-step guidance on how to conduct a course of hypnotherapy, from the initial consultation, through establishing rapport with the client, taking a case history, deciding on the appropriate techniques to use, setting realistic therapy aims and objectives, psycho-education, gathering of therapy resources, induction, deepening, therapeutic intervention, ego strengthening to wakening the patient. There is even a chapter that deals with all aspects of managing a successful therapy practice.